TASTE OF
ASIA

TASTE OF
ASIA

STEVEN WHEELER

Photography by Edward Allwright

SMITHMARK

This edition published in 1994 by
SMITHMARK Publishers Inc.
16 East 32nd Street
New York
NY 10016

Reprinted 1994, 1995

SMITHMARK books are available for bulk purchase for sales
promotion and premium use. For details write or call
the manager of special sales, SMITHMARK Publishers Inc.,
16 East 32nd Street, New York, NY, 10016; (212) 532–0600

ISBN 0 8317 0801 8

Publisher: Joanna Lorenz
Senior Editor: Lindsay Porter
Photography: Edward Allwright
Styling: Maria Kelly
Design: David Rowley Design

Typeset by MC Typeset Ltd.

Printed in Singapore by
Star Standard Industries Pte. Ltd.

Recipes on pages 24–27 by Deh-Ta Hsiung
Recipes on pages 28–29 by Rafi Fernandez

CONTENTS

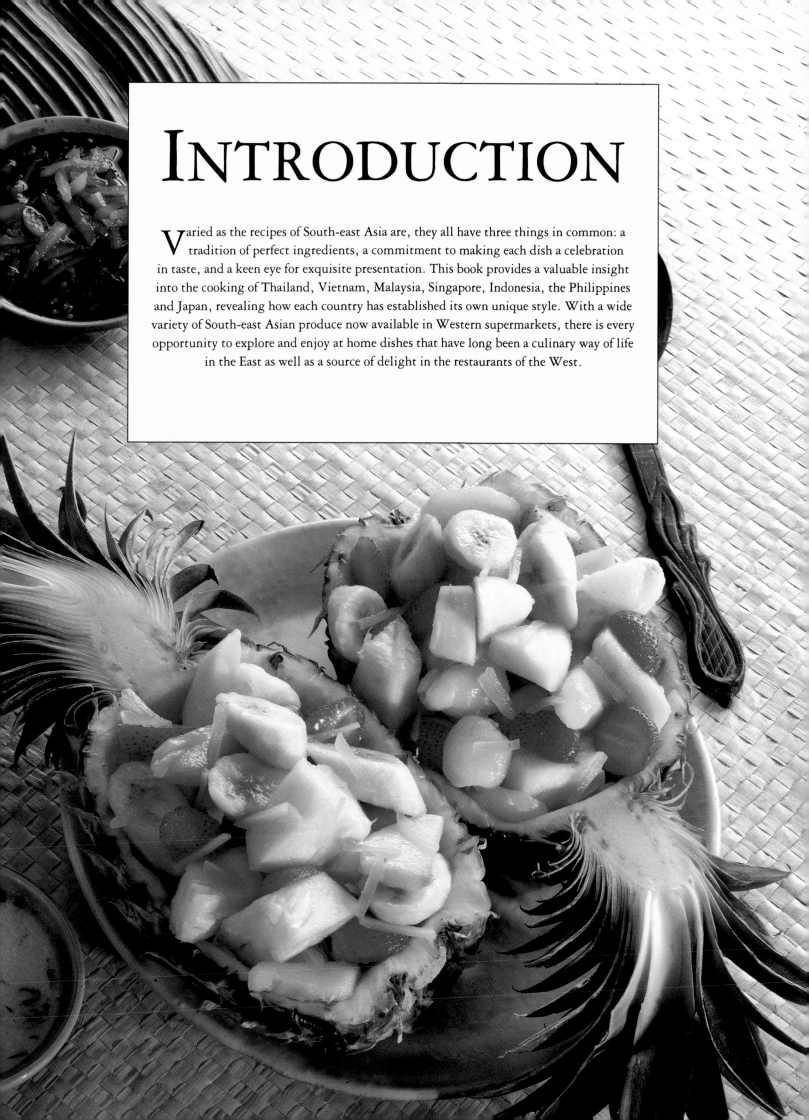

INTRODUCTION

Varied as the recipes of South-east Asia are, they all have three things in common: a tradition of perfect ingredients, a commitment to making each dish a celebration in taste, and a keen eye for exquisite presentation. This book provides a valuable insight into the cooking of Thailand, Vietnam, Malaysia, Singapore, Indonesia, the Philippines and Japan, revealing how each country has established its own unique style. With a wide variety of South-east Asian produce now available in Western supermarkets, there is every opportunity to explore and enjoy at home dishes that have long been a culinary way of life in the East as well as a source of delight in the restaurants of the West.

THE PRINCIPLES OF SOUTHEAST ASIAN COOKING

The cuisines of the countries of Southeast Asia vary considerably, from the Spanish-influenced dishes of the Philippines to the dietary demands of the Buddhist and Muslim faiths. One practice common to most countries is the method of serving. Mealtimes are relaxed, informal affairs, with all dishes arriving at the table at the same time. Guests help themselves, either with chopsticks or by hand. Dishes should offer a balance of textures and aromas, and ingredients must be fresh and flavorsome.

EQUIPMENT AND UTENSILS

Bamboo skewers (1) Bamboo skewers are widely used for barbecues and broiled foods. They are disposed of after use.

Chopping board (2) It is worth investing in a solid chopping board. Thick boards provide the best surface and will last for many years.

Citrus zesting tool (3) The outer peel or zest of citrus fruit imparts a distinctive flavor to many Southeast Asian dishes. This tool is designed to remove the zest while leaving behind the bitter white pith of the fruit.

Cleavers (4, 5) At first sight cleavers may look and feel out of place for domestic use, but they are ideally suited to fine chopping and transferring ingredients from chopping board to wok. Small cleavers are used mostly for chopping and shredding fruits and vegetables. They can also be used for the preparation of meat and fish.

Cooking chopsticks (6) Extra long chopsticks can be used to stir ingredients in the wok. Their length permits you to keep at a distance from the cooking ingredients.

Draining wire (7) Draining wires are designed to rest on the side of a wok. They are used mainly for deep-frying.

Food processor (8) The food processor is a useful alternative to the more traditional pestle and mortar, and is suitable for grinding wet spices.

Large chopping knife (9) If you are not comfortable using a cleaver, a large Western-style chopping knife can be used instead. Choose one with a deep blade to give you the best control.

Rice paddle (10) These are generally made from a large section of bamboo. Rice paddles are used to stir and fluff rice after cooking. A pair of chopsticks can also be used for fluffing rice.

Rice saucepan and lid (11) A good rice saucepan with a close-fitting lid is an essential piece of equipment for Southeast Asian cooking. Stainless steel pans with a heavy base are best.

Sharpening stone (12) Sharpening stones are used for sharpening knives and cleavers. They are available from kitchenware or hardware stores and should be immersed in water before use.

Stainless steel skimmer (13) Stainless steel skimmers should be used when strong flavors are likely to affect bare metal utensils.

Wire skimmer (14) Wire skimmers are used to retrieve cooked food from boiling water or hot fat. Bare metal skimmers can retain strong flavors and are therefore not recommended for use with fish-based liquids.

Wok (15) The wok is used in all parts of Southeast Asia. The shape of the wok allows deep-frying and stir-frying in a minimum of fat, thus retaining the freshness and flavor of ingredients.

Wok ladle (16) Wok ladles are used to stir liquid ingredients while cooking. They are also useful for transferring cooked food to serving bowls.

Wok lid (17) Wok lids have a large domed surface and are designed to retain moisture given off during cooking. The steam held beneath the lid is often used to keep ingredients from taking on too much color when frying.

Wok scoop (18) The wok scoop is designed to make contact with the curved surface of the wok. Most scoops are made of stainless steel and will not retain strong flavors.

INGREDIENTS

Acorn squash (1) Many varieties of squash and pumpkin are grown in Southeast Asia. They are used mainly as a vegetable, but may sometimes be used in desserts.

Banana leaves (3) The banana leaf is widely used for wrapping ingredients before cooking. If banana leaves are unavailable use aluminium foil.

Bean thread noodles (5) These fine noodles are usually made from mung bean flour, although some varieties contain rice, soy, and pea starch. When boiled, they have a smooth texture and are an important ingredient for spring roll stuffings. Bean thread noodles become crispy when deep-fried.

Cardamom pods (4) Cardamom is a member of the ginger family. The sweetest flavor is contained in the seed of the olive-green pods and is usually ground with other spices. Large black pods have a bitter flavor and combine well with sweet curry ingredients.

Chilies (6) Used in moderation, chilies provide the hot sweet glow typical of many Southeast Asian curries and dipping sauces. As a rule, small chilies are the hottest and green varieties tend to be less sweet than red.

Chinese red onions (shallots) (7) The Chinese red onion has a strong flavour despite its small size. If unavailable, use golden shallots or an increased quantity of white onions.

Cilantro (10) Fresh cilantro has a strong, pungent smell that combines well with other rich flavours. The white cilantro root is used when the green coloring is not required. Bunches of cilantro will keep for up to five days in a jar of water. Cover with a plastic bag and store in the refrigerator.

Cinnamon (cassia) (8) Tightly-curled cinnamon has a smooth, warm flavor which is given to sweet and savoury cooking. Cassia, pictured here, has a more robust flavor and is used with other strong spices.

Coconut (9) The coconut is essential to many dishes of Southeast Asia. Coconut milk is obtained from the white flesh of the nut and is both rich and smooth-tasting.

Coriander seeds (11) Coriander is common to all styles of cooking throughout Southeast Asia. The seeds are dry-fried with other spices to release the unique flavor.

Cumin seeds (12) Cumin has a similar ribbed shape to fennel seed and comes from the parsley family. It has a warm, heady flavor that combines well with cilantro and is widely used in beef dishes. Cumin seeds are usually dry-fried before use.

Egg noodles (13) Egg noodles are made from wheat flour and are sold dried in single portions. When cooked, egg noodles are used in dishes such as Mee Goreng from Singapore and Pansit Guisado from the Philippines.

Egg plant (2) The dark-skinned egg plant is included in a variety of slow-cooking dishes and is renowned for its smooth texture. Large egg plant can be bitter and should be salted before use.

Enoki mushrooms (14) These slender mushrooms have a sweet, peppery taste and are used to enhance the clear broths of Japan. Enoki can also be eaten raw as a salad ingredient.

Fennel seeds (15) Plump green fennel seeds are similar in character to cumin, and have a sweet aniseed flavor. The seeds combine well with peanuts and the zest of citrus fruit, and are an aid to digestion.

Fermented shrimp paste (Blachan, Kapi) (16) The smell of fermented shrimp paste by itself is quite repellent, but when blended with other spices, shrimp paste loses its unpleasant flavor and provides the unique taste and character typical of many Southeast Asian sauces.

Galingal (17) Galingal is a member of the ginger family and grows in a similar root shape. The fibrous root has a resinous quality similar to pine and combines well with fish dishes. Dried galingal is increasingly available. It should be soaked in boiling water before use.

Garlic (18) Garlic marries well with the strong pungent flavors of the East. Individual cloves can be finely chopped or crushed in a garlic press.

Ginger (19) Fresh ginger is well known in the West for its warm, pungent flavor. In its native region of Southeast Asia, it features in many intriguing spice combinations.

Lime leaves (20) Lime leaves are an essential part of many slow-cooking dishes. The deep, citrus flavor of the leaf combines especially well with rich coconut milk and hot chili spices.

Limes (21) Limes are widely used to add sharpness to finished dishes. Wedges are often served at the table so that guests may season dishes to taste.

Lemon grass (22) Fresh lemon grass is common to many dishes throughout Southeast Asia. Its flavor has a rich lemon quality that combines well with other wet spices. Lemon grass is also available dried.

Lychees (23) The brittle skin of this fine fruit peels away like the shell of a boiled egg. The white, scented fruit has a clean fresh taste and is served at the end of a meal.

Mandarin oranges (24) The flavor obtained from the outer zest of the mandarin orange combines well with the rich spices of the East. Satsumas and clementines are also suitable.

Mango (25) The mango offers a rich scented flavor to both sweet and savory dishes. Mangoes are ripe when the green skin is flushed with red.

Mint (26) Varieties of mint feature in the cooking of Vietnam. The fresh flavor combines particularly well with cilantro, peanuts, and the zest of mandarin orange. Mint is also used in sweet and savory fruit salads.

Moolie (27) The giant white radish is common to many Japanese dishes and is ideal for making flower garnishes. If unavailable, white turnip or red radish can be substituted.

Nutmeg (28) The flavor of nutmeg is obtained by grating the nut on a fine grater. The fresh oils that are released provide strength and character to many well-known spice mixtures.

Pickled ginger (29) Thinly sliced pink pickled ginger is served as a condiment with Japanese sushi, grilled fish, and beef. It has a warm, sweet flavor and is found in most oriental food stores.

Pineapple (30) Pineapple offers a clean refreshing flavor and is an aid to digestion. It may be served at the end of a meal, or as an ingredient in a main dish.

Scallions (36) Scallions have a milder flavor than onions and are suited to dishes that are cooked quickly. Both the white and green parts are used.

Seaweed (31) Dried seaweed is widely used in Japanese cooking to impart a salty, rich flavor of the sea. Nori is a dried, flat seaweed used for making sushi. Kelp is also dried and should be soaked in water before use.

Sesame seeds (32) White sesame seeds are widely used in Japanese cooking. The seeds should be dry-fried, to release their flavor. Toasted seeds

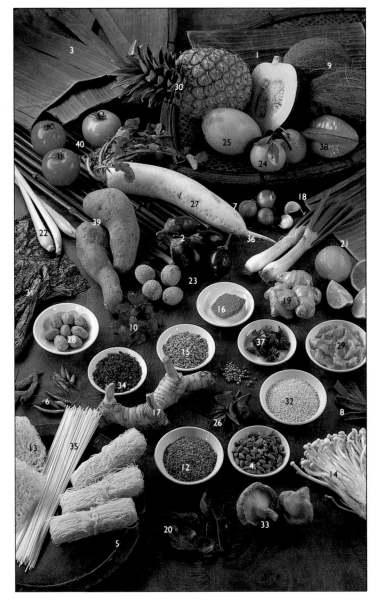

are often ground finely to thicken and enrich sauces.

Shiitaki mushrooms (33) Fresh shiitaki mushrooms have a rich, meaty flavor that combines especially well with shellfish and poultry. Shiitake are widely available dried and yield a good flavor when soaked in boiling water.

Sichuan pepper (34) Sichuan pepper has a warm, fruity flavor without the intense heat of white or black peppercorns. To obtain the best flavor, Sichuan pepper should be dry-fried and coarsely ground before use.

Somen noodles (35) Somen noodles are made from wheat flour and are an important part of the Japanese diet. It is most common to find somen noodles in a flavorsome chicken broth.

Star anise (37) This attractive spice is sold in star-shaped pods and carries the soft scent of aniseed. The pods are used whole or ground to flavor sweet and savory dishes.

Star fruit (38) Star fruit have a sweet scented flavor when ripe and can be eaten cooked or raw in fruit salads.

Sweet potato (39) The sweet richness of this red tuber marries well with the hot and sour flavors of Southeast Asia. In Japan, the sweet potato is used to make delicious candies.

Tomatoes (40) Both ripe and under-ripe tomatoes feature in the cooking of Southeast Asia. Under-ripe fruit are used in slow-cooking meat dishes and lend a special sour taste.

THAILAND

HOT CHILI DUCK WITH CRABMEAT AND CASHEW NUT SAUCE

Bhed Sune Khan

This dish may be served with Thai rice and a dish of Thai Dipping Sauce.

SERVES 4–6	5 tsp sugar	4 shallots, or I medium onion, finely chopped
	½ tsp salt	I piece shrimp paste, ¾in square
Ingredients	2 tbsp coriander seeds	Ioz cilantro, white root or stem, finely
6lb duck	I tsp caraway seeds	chopped
5 cups water, to cover	4oz raw cashew nuts, chopped	6oz frozen white crabmeat, thawed
2 lime leaves	I piece lemon grass, 3in long, shredded	2oz unsweetened cream of coconut
I tsp salt	I piece galingal or fresh ginger, Iin long, peeled	I small bunch cilantro, chopped, to garnish
2–3 small red chilies, seeded and finely	and finely chopped	
chopped	2 cloves garlic, crushed	

1 To portion the duck into manageable pieces, first remove the legs. Separate the thighs from the drumsticks and chop each thigh and drumstick into 2 pieces. Trim away the lower half of the duck with kitchen scissors. Cut the breast piece in half down the middle, then chop each half into 4 pieces.

2 Put the duck flesh and bones into a large saucepan and cover with the water. Add the lime leaves and salt, bring to a boil and simmer, uncovered, for 35–40 minutes, until the meat is tender. Discard the duck bones, skim off the fat from the stock, and set aside.

3 To make the curry sauce, grind the red chilies together with the sugar and salt using a pestle and mortar or a food processor. Dry-fry the coriander and caraway seeds and the cashew nuts in a wok to release their flavor, about 1–2 minutes. Add the chilies, the lemon grass, galingal or ginger, garlic, and shallots or onion, and reduce to a smooth paste. Add the shrimp paste and cilantro.

4 Add 1 cup of the liquid in which the duck was cooked and blend until a thin paste is obtained.

5 Stir the curry seasoning in with the duck, bring to a boil, and simmer, uncovered, for 20–25 minutes.

6 Add the crabmeat and cream of coconut and simmer briefly. Turn out onto an attractive serving dish, decorate with cilantro and serve.

THAI BROILED CHICKEN

Kai Yang

Thai grilled chicken is especially delicious when cooked on the barbecue. It should be served with a dipping sauce.

SERVES 4–6	4 tsp sugar	3 tbsp vegetable oil
	2 tsp paprika	salt, to season
Ingredients	1 piece fresh ginger, ¾in long	6–8 lettuce leaves, to serve
2lb chicken drumsticks or thighs	3 cloves garlic, crushed	½ cucumber, cut into strips, to garnish
1 tsp whole black peppercorns	½oz cilantro, white root or stem,	4 scallions, trimmed, to garnish
½ tsp caraway or cumin seeds	finely chopped	2 limes, quartered, to garnish

1 Chop through the narrow end of each drumstick with a heavy knife. Score the chicken pieces deeply to allow the marinade to penetrate. Set aside in a shallow bowl.

2 Grind the peppercorns, caraway or cumin seeds, and sugar in a pestle and mortar or a food processor. Add the paprika, ginger, garlic, cilantro, and oil and grind or process.

3 Spread over the marinade and chill for 6 hours. Cook under the broiler for 20 minutes, or until cooked through, turning once. Season, arrange on lettuce, and garnish.

THAI CHICKEN AND SHRIMP SOUP

Tom Yum Gung

In Thailand a soup such as this is often served with a dry curry to help balance the texture of the curry dish.

SERVES 4–6	1 piece lemon grass, 3in long	2 lime leaves
	2 cloves garlic, crushed	8oz fresh or cooked shrimp tails, peeled and
Ingredients	2 tbsp chopped cilantro root, or stem	deveined
6oz chicken breasts, on the bone	2–3 small red chilies, seeded and finely	juice of 1 lime
½ chicken stock cube	chopped	4 sprigs cilantro, chopped, to garnish
14oz canned coconut milk	2 tbsp fish sauce	2 scallions, green part only, sliced, to garnish
1 piece galingal or fresh ginger, ¾in long,	5 tsp sugar	4 large red chilies, sliced, to garnish
finely chopped	½ tsp salt	

1 Cover the chicken with water, add stock cube, and simmer for 45 minutes. Slice the meat into strips (discard skin), and return to stock. Add coconut milk and simmer.

2 Blend the lemon grass, galingal or ginger, garlic, cilantro and chilies. Add this to the stock with the fish sauce, sugar, salt, and lime leaves. Simmer for 20 minutes.

3 Just before serving, add the shrimp and lime juice. Simmer for 5 minutes. Decorate with the cilantro, scallions and chilies.

DRY BEEF CURRY WITH PEANUT AND LIME

Nua Pad Prik

Dry curries originated from the mountainous northern regions of Thailand but are popular throughout the country. This dry beef curry is usually served with a moist dish such as Ragout of Shellfish with Sweet Scented Basil, or Thai Chicken and Shrimp Soup. The curry is equally delicious made with a lean leg or shoulder of lamb.

SERVES 4–6

Ingredients
2lb stewing beef, (chuck is best), finely chopped
14oz canned coconut milk
1¼ cups beef stock

Red curry paste
2 tbsp coriander seeds
1 tsp cumin seeds
6 green cardamom pods, seeds only
½ tsp ground nutmeg
¼ tsp ground clove
½ tsp ground cinnamon
4 tsp paprika
zest of 1 mandarin orange, finely chopped
4–5 small red chilies, seeded and finely chopped
5 tsp sugar
½ tsp salt
1 piece lemon grass, 4in long, shredded
3 cloves garlic, crushed
1 piece galingal or fresh ginger, ¾in long, peeled and finely chopped
4 red shallots or 1 medium red onion, finely chopped
1 piece shrimp paste, ¾in square
2oz cilantro, white root or stem, chopped
juice of 2½ limes
2 tbsp vegetable oil
2 tbsp chunky peanut butter
1 lime, sliced, to garnish
1 large red chili, sliced, to garnish
1 small bunch cilantro, shredded, to garnish

---

1 Place the meat in the freezer for 30–40 minutes until firm. Slice the meat thinly, cut into strips, and chop finely. Strain the coconut milk into a bowl.

2 Place the thin part and half of the thick part of the milk in a large saucepan. Add the beef, and beef stock, bring to a boil, cover, and simmer for 50 minutes.

3 To make the curry paste, dry-fry the coriander, cumin seeds, and cardamom in a wok for 1–2 minutes. Combine with the nutmeg, clove, cinnamon, paprika, and the zest of the mandarin orange. Pound the chilies with the sugar and salt. Add the chili paste, lemon grass, garlic, galingal or ginger, shallots or onion, and shrimp paste. Lastly add the cilantro, juice of ½ lime, and oil.

4 Place a cupful of the cooking liquid in a wok, and add 2–3 tbsp of the curry paste according to taste. Boil rapidly until the liquid has reduced completely. Add the remainder of the coconut milk, the peanut butter, and the beef. Simmer, uncovered, for 15–20 minutes. Stir in the remaining lime juice. Serve decorated with the lime, chili and cilantro.

GREEN CURRY-COCONUT CHICKEN

Kaeng Khieu Wan Gai

The recipe given here for green curry paste is a complex one and therefore takes time to make properly. Pork, shrimp and fish can all be used instead of chicken, but cooking times must be adjusted accordingly.

SERVES 4–6

Ingredients
2½lb chicken, without giblets
2½ cups canned coconut milk
1½ cups chicken stock
2 lime leaves

Green curry paste
2 tsp coriander seeds

½ tsp caraway or cumin seeds
3–4 medium green chilies, finely chopped
4 tsp sugar
2 tsp salt
1 piece lemon grass, 3in long
1 piece galingal or fresh ginger, ¾in long, peeled and finely chopped
3 cloves garlic, crushed
4 shallots or 1 medium onion, finely chopped
1 piece shrimp paste, ¾in square

3 tbsp cilantro leaves, finely chopped
3 tbsp fresh mint or basil, finely chopped
½ tsp nutmeg powder
2 tbsp vegetable oil
12oz sweet potatoes, peeled and roughly chopped
12oz winter squash, peeled, seeded, and roughly chopped
4oz French green beans, topped, tailed and halved
1 small bunch cilantro, shredded, to garnish

---

1 To prepare the chicken, remove the legs, then separate the thighs from the drumsticks. Separate the lower part of the chicken carcass by cutting through the rib section with kitchen scissors. Divide the breast part in half down the middle, then chop each half in two. Remove skin from all pieces and set aside.

2 Strain the coconut milk into a bowl, reserving the thick part. Place the chicken in a stainless steel or enamel saucepan, cover with the thin part of the coconut milk and the stock. Add the lime leaves, and simmer, uncovered, for 40 minutes. Remove the chicken from the bone and set aside.

3 Dry-fry the coriander and caraway or cumin seeds. Grind the chilies with the sugar and salt to make a smooth paste. Combine the seeds from the wok with the chilies, the lemon grass, galingal or ginger, garlic, and shallots, then grind smoothly. Add the next 5 ingredients.

4 Place a cupful of the cooking liquid in a large wok. Add 4–5 tbsp of the curry paste to the liquid according to taste. Boil rapidly until the liquid has reduced completely. Add the chicken stock, chicken meat, sweet potatoes, squash, and beans. Simmer for 10–15 minutes until the potatoes are cooked. Just before serving, stir in the thick part of the coconut milk and simmer until thick. Serve decorated with the shredded cilantro.

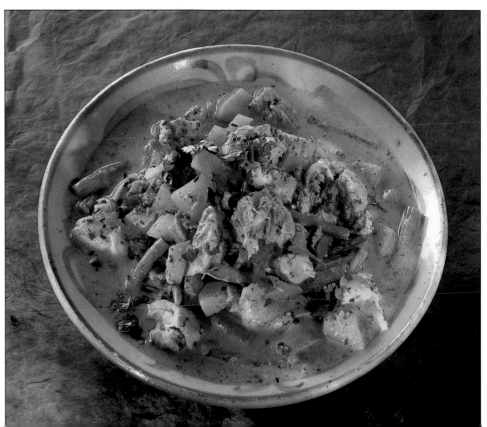

THAI STEAMED FISH WITH A CITRUS MARINADE

Pla Chien

Serve Thai rice or fine rice noodles as an accompaniment to this dish.

SERVES 4–6

Ingredients
3lb parrot fish, pomfret, plaice, or sea bream,
    gutted with heads on
2 small red chilies, seeded and finely
    chopped
1 tbsp sugar
2 cloves garlic, crushed
3 scallions, white part only, chopped
1 piece fresh galingal or fresh ginger, 1 in long,
    peeled and finely chopped
juice of 1 mandarin orange
zest of 1 mandarin orange, finely chopped
1 tbsp tamarind sauce
1 tbsp fish sauce
2 tbsp light soy sauce
juice of 1 lime
1 tbsp vegetable oil
2 limes, quartered, to garnish
4 scallion curls, to garnish

1 Wash the fish thoroughly and score 3–4 times with a sharp knife on each side to allow the marinade to penetrate deeply. Place the fish in a shallow dish that will fit in the base of a steamer. You can also wrap the fish loosely in foil.

2 Grind the chili and sugar together using a pestle and mortar or food processor, add the garlic, scallion, galingal or ginger, and the zest of the mandarin orange. Combine well. Lastly add the tamarind, fish and soy sauces, the lime juice, and vegetable oil, then spread evenly over the fish. Leave to marinate for at least 1 hour.

3 Cook the fish in a covered steamer for 25–30 minutes. Lift the fish onto a serving plate and decorate with wedges of lime and the scallion curls.

PORK AND PEANUT PICK-ME-UPS

Ma Hor

With a Thai meal, it is not customary to have a starter. Instead, appetizers are served with drinks beforehand.

MAKES 12

Ingredients
1 tbsp vegetable oil
2 shallots, or 1 small onion, finely chopped
1 clove garlic, crushed
1 piece fresh ginger, ¾in long, peeled and finely
    chopped

1 small red chili, seeded and finely chopped
5oz ground pork, or 5oz fresh pork sausage meat
2 tbsp peanut butter
1 tbsp fish sauce
juice of ½ lime
4 tsp sugar
2 tbsp chopped cilantro leaves
4 clementines, peeled and thickly sliced

6 ramboutans, or lychees, peeled and pitted
1 small pineapple, peeled, cored, and sliced
1 firm pear, peeled, cored, and sliced
1 lime, cut into small wedges, to garnish
12 cilantro leaves, to garnish

1 Heat the oil and fry the next 4 ingredients. Add the pork and cook for 10 minutes.

2 Add the peanut butter, fish sauce, lime juice, sugar, and chopped cilantro.

3 Spoon the topping onto pieces of fruit. Decorate with lime and cilantro leaves.

THAI DIPPING SAUCE

Nam Prik

Nam Prik is the most common dipping sauce in Thailand. It has a fiery strength, so use with caution.

MAKES ½ CUP

Ingredients
1 tbsp vegetable oil
1 piece shrimp paste, ½in square, or
  1 tbsp fish sauce
2 cloves garlic, finely sliced
1 piece fresh ginger, ¾in long, peeled and finely
  chopped
3 small red chilies, seeded and chopped
1 tbsp finely chopped cilantro root or stem
4 tsp sugar
3 tbsp dark soy sauce
juice of ½ lime

1 Heat the vegetable oil in a wok, add the shrimp paste or fish sauce, garlic, ginger, and chilies and soften without coloring, for about 1–2 minutes.

2 Remove from the heat and add the cilantro, sugar, soy sauce, and lime juice. Nam Prik Sauce will keep in an airtight container for up to 10 days.

HOT COCONUT SHRIMP AND PAW PAW SALAD

Yam Ma-La-Kaw Prik

This dish may be served as an accompaniment to beef and chicken dishes.

SERVES 4–6

Ingredients
8oz fresh or cooked shrimp tails, peeled and
  deveined
2 ripe paw paws, or papayas
8oz lettuce leaves, Napa cabbage and young
  spinach

1 firm tomato, skinned, seeded, and roughly
  chopped
3 scallions, shredded

Dressing
3 tbsp unsweetened cream of coconut
6 tbsp vegetable oil
juice of 1 lime

½ tsp hot chili sauce
2 tsp fish sauce (optional)
1 tsp sugar
1 small bunch cilantro, shredded, to garnish
1 large chili, sliced, to garnish

1 To make the dressing, place the cream of coconut in a screw-top jar and add the vegetable oil, lime juice, chili sauce, fish sauce if using, and sugar. Shake well and set aside. Do not refrigerate.

2 If using fresh shrimp tails, cover with cold water in a saucepan, bring to a boil, and simmer for no longer than 2 minutes. Drain and set aside.

3 To prepare the paw paws or papayas, cut each in half from top to bottom and remove the black seeds with a spoon. Peel away the outer skin and cut the flesh into even-sized pieces. Wash the salad leaves and toss in a bowl. Add the other ingredients. Pour on the dressing and serve.

RED CURRY BEEF WITH TAMARIND

Kang Mussaman Nuea

This red curry can also be made using diced lamb, in which case reduce the cooking time by 30 minutes.

SERVES 4–6	4 tsp paprika	12oz new potatoes, peeled and roughly chopped
	zest of 1 mandarin orange, finely chopped	12oz pumpkin or winter squash
Ingredients	4–5 small red chilies, seeded and finely chopped	7oz canned bamboo shoots, sliced
2lb stewing beef (chuck is best)	5 tsp sugar	2 tbsp smooth peanut butter
14oz canned coconut milk	½ tsp salt	2 tbsp tamarind sauce
1¼ cups beef stock	1 piece lemon grass, 4in long, shredded	juice of 2 limes
	3 cloves garlic, crushed	1 small bunch cilantro, to garnish
Red curry paste	1 piece galingal or fresh ginger, ¾in long, peeled	
2 tbsp coriander seeds	and finely chopped	
1 tsp cumin seeds	4 red shallots or 1 medium red onion, finely	
6 green cardamom pods, seeds only	chopped	
½ tsp ground nutmeg	1 piece shrimp paste, ¾in square	
¼ tsp ground cloves	2oz cilantro, white root or stem, chopped	
½ tsp ground cinnamon	2 tbsp vegetable oil	

1 Cut the beef into 1in dice and place in a stainless steel saucepan.

2 Place the coconut milk in a fine strainer and allow the liquid to drain into a bowl. Add all of the liquid and half of the coconut milk solids to the saucepan. Add the stock, bring to a boil, and simmer, uncovered, for 1 hour. Strain and set aside.

3 Dry-fry the coriander, cumin seeds, and cardamom in a wok for 1–2 minutes. Combine with the nutmeg, clove, cinnamon, paprika and mandarin zest, and grind. Pound the chilies with the sugar and salt. Add the chili paste, lemon grass, garlic, galingal, shallots, and shrimp paste. Add the cilantro and oil and reduce.

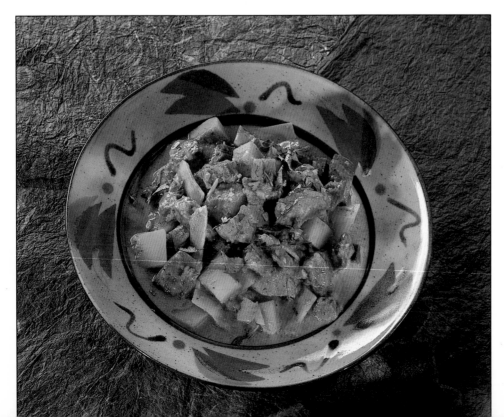

4 Place a cupful of the cooking liquid in a large wok. Add 2–3 tbsp of the paste. Boil rapidly to reduce the liquid. Add the peanut butter and tamarind sauce. Add the beef, potatoes, pumpkin, and bamboo shoots and simmer for 20–25 minutes until the potatoes are cooked. Stir in the coconut milk solids and the lime juice. Return to a gentle simmer. Decorate, and serve with Thai rice.

COCONUT MILK

Coconut milk is used to enrich and flavor many dishes in the Far East. Only the Japanese choose not to include it in their cooking. Coconut milk is not, as many suppose, the liquid found inside the nut. Although this thin liquid does make a refreshing drink, the coconut milk used for cooking is processed from the white flesh of the nut. If left to stand, the thick part of the milk will rise to the surface like cream. If the milk is cold the thick part of the milk will separate more easily. Choose a coconut with plenty of milk inside. Shake the nut firmly. If you cannot hear the milk sloshing around, the flesh will be difficult to remove. If you can find a coconut with its green husk and fibre attached, the flesh will almost certainly be soft and creamy white. Fresh coconut milk will keep in a cool place for up to 10 days. If kept in the refrigerator, allow to soften at room temperature before using.

MAKES 1¾ cups

Ingredients
2 fresh coconuts
5 cups water, just boiled

1 Hold the coconut over a bowl to collect the liquid. With the back of a large knife or cleaver, crack open the coconut by striking it cleanly.

2 Scrape out the white meat with a citrus zester or a rounded butter curler. Place the coconut meat in a food processor with half of the water.

3 Process for 1 minute, then pass through a food mill fitted with a fine disk, catching the milk in a bowl beneath. Alternatively, squeeze the coconut meat with your hands and press through a nylon strainer. Return the coconut meat to the mill or food processor with the remainder of the water, blend, and press for a second time. Allow the milk to settle for 30 minutes (creamy solids will rise to the surface). Sometimes the solids should be poured off and added later as a thickener.

Cook's tip

Coconut milk can be obtained directly from coconut flesh – this gives the creamiest milk. It is also available in a can, as a soluble powder, and in block form. Coconut milk which is pre-packaged in this way makes a useful addition to sauces and dressings.

RAGOUT OF SHELLFISH WITH SWEET SCENTED BASIL

Po-Tak

Green curry paste can be used to accompany other dishes, such as Green Curry-Coconut Chicken. Curry pastes will keep for up to 3 weeks in the refrigerator if stored in an airtight container.

SERVES 4–6	**Green curry paste**	2 tbsp vegetable oil
	2 tsp coriander seeds	4 sprigs large-leaf basil, torn, to garnish
Ingredients	½ tsp caraway or cumin seeds	
2½ cups fresh mussels in their shells, cleaned	3–4 medium green chilies, finely chopped	
8oz medium cuttle fish or squid	4 tsp sugar	
12oz monkfish, hokey, or red snapper, skinned	2 tsp salt	
5oz fresh or cooked shrimp tails, peeled and	1 piece lemon grass, 3in long	
deveined	1 piece galingal or fresh ginger, ¾in long, peeled	
4 scallops, sliced (optional)	and finely chopped	
14oz canned coconut milk	3 cloves garlic, crushed	
1¼ cups chicken or vegetable stock	4 shallots or 1 medium onion, finely chopped	
3oz green beans, trimmed and cooked	1 piece shrimp paste, ¾in square	
2oz canned bamboo shoots, drained	2oz cilantro leaves, finely chopped	
1 ripe tomato, skinned, seeded, and roughly	3 tbsp fresh mint or basil, finely chopped	
chopped	½ tsp ground nutmeg	

1   Place the mussels in a stainless steel or enamel saucepan, add 4 tbsp of water, cover, steam open and cook for 6–8 minutes. Take ¾ of the mussels out of their shells (discard any which don't open), strain the cooking liquid, and set aside.

2   To prepare the cuttle fish or squid, trim off the tentacles beneath the eye. Rinse under cold running water, discarding the gut. Remove the cuttle shell from inside the body and rub off the paper-thin skin. Cut the body open and score, criss-cross, with a sharp knife. Cut into strips and set aside.

3   To make the green curry paste, dry-fry the coriander and caraway or cumin seeds in a wok to release their flavour. Grind the chilies with the sugar and salt using a pestle and mortar or food processor to make a smooth paste. Combine the seeds from the wok with the chilies, add the lemon grass, galingal or ginger, garlic, and shallots or onion, then grind smoothly. Add the shrimp paste, cilantro, mint or basil, nutmeg, and vegetable oil. Combine well. There may seem to be a lot of cilantro and mint at this stage, but their volume will reduce considerably when ground with the other spices.

4   Pour the coconut milk into a strainer. Pour the thin part of the milk together with the chicken or vegetable stock into a wok. The coconut milk solids are added later. Add 4–5 tbsp of the green curry paste according to taste. You can add more paste later if you need to. Boil rapidly until the liquid has reduced completely.

5   Add the coconut milk solids, then add the cuttle fish or squid and monkfish, hokey or red snapper. Simmer, uncovered, for 15–20 minutes. Then add the shrimp, scallops, and cooked mussels with the beans, bamboo shoots, and tomato. Simmer for 2–3 minutes, transfer to a bowl, and decorate with the basil and chilies.

BRAISED WHOLE FISH IN CHILI AND GARLIC SAUCE

Gan Shao Yu

This recipe reflects its Chinese origins. When served in a restaurant, the fish's head and tail are usually discarded before cooking, and used in other dishes. A whole fish may be used, however, and always looks impressive, especially for formal occasions and dinner parties.

SERVES 4–6

Ingredients
1 carp, bream, sea bass, trout, grouper or striped mullet, weighing about 1½lb, gutted
1 tbsp light soy sauce
1 tbsp rice wine or dry sherry
vegetable oil, for deep-frying

1 tsp finely chopped fresh ginger
2 tbsp hot bean sauce
1 tbsp tomato paste
2 tsp light brown sugar
1 tbsp rice vinegar
about ½ cup stock
1 tbsp cornstarch paste
few drops sesame oil

Sauce
2 cloves garlic, finely chopped
2–3 scallions, finely chopped with the white and green parts separated

1 Rinse and dry the fish well. Using a sharp knife, score both sides of the fish as far down as the bone with diagonal cuts about 1in apart. Rub the whole fish with soy sauce, and wine or sherry on both sides, then leave to marinate for 10–15 minutes.

2 In a wok, deep-fry the fish in hot oil for about 3–4 minutes on both sides or until golden brown.

3 Pour off the excess oil, leaving about 1 tbsp in the wok. Push the fish to one side of the wok and add the garlic, the white part of the scallions, ginger, hot bean sauce, tomato paste, sugar, vinegar, and stock. Bring to a boil and braise the fish in the sauce for 4–5 minutes, turning it over once. Add the green part of the scallions. Thicken the sauce with the cornstarch paste, sprinkle with the sesame oil, and serve.

STEAMED FISH WITH GINGER AND SCALLIONS

Qing Zheng Yu

Any firm-fleshed fish with a delicate taste, such as salmon or turbot, can be cooked by this same method. The sweet taste of ginger combines with the scallions to make this a highly distinctive dish. It originated in mainland China.

SERVES 4–6

Ingredients
1 sea bass, trout or striped mullet, weighing about 1½lb, gutted
½ tsp salt
1 tbsp sesame oil
2–3 scallions, cut in half lengthwise
2 tbsp light soy sauce
2 tbsp rice wine or dry sherry
1 tbsp finely shredded fresh ginger
2 tbsp vegetable oil
finely shredded scallions, to garnish

1 Using a sharp knife, score both sides of the fish as far down as the bone, making several diagonal cuts about 1in apart. Rub the fish all over, inside and out, with salt and sesame oil.

2 Sprinkle the scallions on a heatproof platter and place the fish on top. Blend together the soy sauce, and wine or sherry with the ginger shreds and pour all over the fish.

3 Place the platter in a very hot steamer (or inside a wok on a rack), and steam vigorously, covered, for 12–15 minutes.

4 Heat the oil until hot; remove the platter from the steamer, place the shredded scallions on top of the fish, then pour the hot oil along the whole length of the fish. Serve immediately.

RED AND WHITE SHRIMP WITH GREEN VEGETABLES

Yuan Yang Xia

Rice and salad are the ideal accompaniments to this Chinese-influenced recipe. The name of the dish is similar in meaning to 'love birds', symbolizing affection and happiness.

SERVES 4–6

Ingredients
1lb uncooked shrimp
pinch of salt
½ egg white
1 tbsp cornstarch paste
6oz snow peas
about 2½ cups vegetable oil
½ tsp salt

1 tsp light brown sugar
1 tbsp finely chopped scallions
1 tsp finely chopped fresh ginger
1 tbsp light soy sauce
1 tbsp rice wine or dry sherry
1 tsp hot bean sauce
1 tbsp tomato paste

1 Peel and devein the shrimp, and mix with the pinch of salt, the egg white, and the cornstarch paste. Top and tail the snow peas.

2 Heat about 2–3 tbsp of the oil in a preheated wok and stir-fry the snow peas for about 1 minute, then add the salt and sugar and continue stirring for 1 minute more. Remove and place in the center of a warmed serving platter.

3 Heat the remaining oil, partially cook the shrimp for 1 minute, remove, and drain on paper towels.

4 Pour off the excess oil, leaving about 1 tbsp in the wok, and add the scallions and ginger to flavor the oil.

5 Add the shrimp and stir-fry for about 1 minute, then add the soy sauce and wine or sherry. Blend well and place about half of the shrimp at one end of the platter.

6 Add the hot bean sauce and tomato paste to the remaining shrimp in the wok. Blend well and place the 'red' shrimp at the other end of the platter. Serve immediately.

Shrimp Cooked with Okra

Jingha Aur Bhendi

This dish has a sweet taste with a strong chili flavor. It should be cooked fast to prevent the okra from breaking up and releasing its distinctive, sticky interior.

SERVES 4–6

Ingredients
4–6 tbsp oil
8oz okra, washed, dried, and left whole
4 cloves garlic, crushed
1 piece fresh ginger, 2in long, crushed
4–6 green chilies, cut diagonally
½ tsp turmeric
4–6 curry leaves
1 tsp cumin seeds
1lb fresh jumbo shrimp, peeled and deveined
salt, to taste
2 tsp brown sugar
juice of 2 lemons

1 Heat the oil in a frying pan and fry the okra on a moderately high heat until they are slightly crisp and browned on all sides. Remove them from the oil and set aside on paper towels.

2 In the same oil, gently fry the garlic, ginger, chilies, turmeric, curry leaves, and cumin seeds for 2–3 minutes. Add the shrimp and mix well. Cook until the shrimp are tender.

3 Add the salt, sugar, lemon juice, and fried okra. Increase the heat and fry quickly for 5 minutes more, stirring gently to prevent the okra from breaking. Adjust the seasoning, if necessary. Serve hot.

Fried Whole Fish

Tali Huvey Macchi

Rice and a dipping sauce are the perfect table partners to this dish which has origins that can be traced back to the shores of Southern India.

SERVES 4–6

Ingredients
1 small onion, coarsely chopped
4 cloves garlic, peeled
1 piece fresh ginger, 2in long, peeled
1 tsp turmeric
2 tsp chili powder
salt, to taste
4 red mullets
vegetable oil, for shallow-frying
1 tsp cumin seeds
3 green chilies, finely sliced
lemon or lime wedges, to serve

1 Using a food processor, grind the first 6 ingredients to a smooth paste. Make gashes on both sides of the fish and rub them with the paste. Leave to rest for 1 hour. Lightly pat the fish dry with paper towels without removing the paste. Excess fluid will be released as the salt dissolves.

2 Heat the oil in a large frying pan and fry the cumin seeds and chilies for about 1 minute. Add the fish and fry on one side without overlapping. When the first side is seared, turn the fish over very gently to ensure they do not break. Fry until they are golden brown on both sides, drain well, and serve hot with lemon or lime wedges.

Thai Fruit and Vegetable Salad

Yam Chomphu

This fruit salad is presented with the main course and serves as a cooler to counteract the heat of the chilies.

SERVES 4–6

Ingredients
1 small pineapple
1 small mango, peeled and sliced
1 green apple, cored and sliced
6 ramboutans or lychees, peeled and pitted
4oz green beans, trimmed, and halved
1 medium red onion, sliced
1 small cucumber, cut into short fingers
4oz bean sprouts
2 scallions, sliced

1 ripe tomato, quartered
8oz romaine, bib, or iceberg lettuce leaves

Coconut dipping sauce
5 tbsp unsweetened cream of coconut
2 tbsp sugar
¼ tsp chili sauce
1 tbsp fish sauce
juice of 1 lime

Cook's tip

Creamed coconut is sold in 7oz blocks and may be found in specialist food stores. In warm weather, creamed coconut should be stored in a cool place to keep it from softening. To use, soften with boiling water to achieve a creamy consistency. Canned cream of coconut can also be used, but make sure you buy the unsweetened variety.

1 To make the coconut dipping sauce, measure the coconut, sugar, and boiling water into a screw-top jar. Add the chili and fish sauces and lime juice and shake.

2 Trim both ends of the pineapple with a serrated knife, then cut away the outer skin. Remove the central core with an apple corer. Alternatively, cut the pineapple into 4 down the middle and remove the core with a knife. Roughly chop the pineapple and set aside with the other fruits.

3 Bring a small saucepan of salted water to the boil and cook the beans for 3–4 minutes. Refresh under cold running water and set aside. To serve, arrange the fruits and vegetables into small heaps in a shallow bowl. Serve the coconut sauce separately as a dip.

Sweet Cucumber Cooler

Ajad

Sweet dipping sauces such as this bring instant relief to the hot chili flavors of Thai food.

MAKES ½ CUP

Ingredients
5 tbsp water
2 tbsp sugar
½ tsp salt
1 tbsp rice or white wine vinegar
¼ small cucumber, quartered and thinly sliced
2 shallots, or 1 small red onion, thinly sliced

1 Measure the water, sugar, salt, and vinegar into a stainless steel or enamel saucepan. Bring to a boil and simmer until the sugar has dissolved, not more than 1 minute.

2 Allow to cool. Add the cucumber and shallots or onion and serve at room temperature.

HONEY-GLAZED QUAIL WITH A FIVE-SPICE MARINADE

Bo Can Quay

Chinese supermarkets sell five-spice powder in packets. Provided the blend is not kept for longer than 3 months, the flavor can be good, and a useful alternative to making your own.

SERVES 4–6

Ingredients
4 quails, cleaned
2 pieces star anise
2 tsp ground cinnamon
2 tsp fennel seeds
2 tsp Sichuan or Chinese pepper
a pinch ground cloves
1 small onion, finely chopped
1 clove garlic, crushed
4 tbsp clear honey
2 tbsp dark soy sauce
2 roughly chopped scallions, to garnish
mandarin orange or satsuma, to garnish
banana leaves, to serve

1 Remove the backbones from the quails by cutting down either side with a pair of kitchen scissors.

2 Flatten the birds with the palm of your hand and firmly secure each bird using 2 bamboo skewers.

3 Place the five spices in a pestle and mortar or spice mill and grind into a fine powder. Add the onion, garlic, honey, and soy sauce, and combine well.

4 Place the quails in a flat dish, cover with the marinade, and leave for at least 8 hours for the flavors to mingle.

5 Preheat the broiler or a barbecue to a moderate temperature and cook the quails for 7–8 minutes on each side, basting occasionally with the marinade.

6 To garnish, remove the outer zest from the mandarin orange or satsuma with a vegetable peeler or a zesting tool. Shred the zest finely and combine with the chopped scallions. Arrange the quails on a bed of banana leaves, garnish with the orange zest and scallions, and serve.

Hot Chili Chicken with Ginger and Lemon-Grass

Ga Xao Xa Ot

This dish can also be prepared using duck legs. Be sure to remove the jointed parts of the drumsticks and thigh bones to make the meat easier to eat with chopsticks.

SERVES 4–6

Ingredients
3 chicken legs (thighs and drumsticks)
1 tbsp vegetable oil
1 piece fresh ginger, ¾in long, peeled and finely chopped

1 clove garlic, crushed
1 small red chili, seeded and finely chopped
1 piece lemon grass, 2in long, shredded
⅔ cup chicken stock
1 tbsp fish sauce (optional)
2 tsp sugar
½ tsp salt

juice of ½ lemon
2oz raw peanuts
2 scallions, shredded
1 zest of mandarin orange or satsuma, shredded
2 tbsp chopped mint
rice or rice noodles, to serve

---

1 With the heel of the knife, chop through the narrow end of the drumsticks. Remove the jointed parts of the drumsticks and thigh bones, then remove the skin.

2 Heat the oil in a large wok or frying pan. Add the chicken, ginger, garlic, chili and lemongrass and cook for 3–4 minutes. Add the chicken stock, fish sauce if using, sugar, salt, and lemon juice. Cover and simmer gently for 30–35 minutes.

3 To prepare the peanuts for the topping, the red skin must be removed. To do this, broil or roast the peanuts under a steady heat until evenly brown, for about 2–3 minutes. Transfer the nuts to a clean cloth and rub briskly to loosen the skins.

4 Serve the chicken scattered with roasted peanuts, shredded scallions, and the zest of the mandarin orange or satsuma. Serve with rice or rice noodles.

CRAB, PORK, AND MUSHROOM SPRING ROLLS

Cha Gio

If you cannot obtain ground pork, use the meat from the equivalent weight of best-quality pork sausages. Filled spring rolls can be made in advance and kept in the refrigerator ready for frying.

MAKES 12 ROLLS

Ingredients
1oz rice noodles
2oz Chinese mushrooms (shiitake), fresh or dried
1 tbsp vegetable oil
4 scallions, chopped
1 small carrot, grated
6oz ground pork
4oz white crabmeat

1 tsp fish sauce (optional)
salt and pepper
12 frozen spring roll skins, defrosted
2 tbsp cornstarch paste
vegetable oil, for deep-frying
1 head iceberg or bibb lettuce, to serve
1 bunch mint or basil, to serve
1 bunch cilantro leaves, to serve
½ hothouse cucumber, sliced, to serve

1 Bring a large saucepan of salted water to the boil, and simmer the noodles for 8 minutes. Cut the noodles into finger-length pieces. If the mushrooms are dried, soak them in boiling water for about 10 minutes before slicing thinly.

2 To make the filling, heat the oil in a wok or frying pan, add the scallions, carrot, and pork and cook for 8–10 minutes. Remove from the heat, then add the crabmeat, fish sauce, and seasoning. Add the noodles and mushrooms, and set aside.

3 To fill the rolls, brush one spring roll skin at a time with the cornstarch paste, then place 1 tsp of the filling onto the skin. Fold the edges towards the middle and roll evenly to make a neat cigar shape. The paste will help seal the wrapper.

4 Heat the oil in a wok or deep-fryer until hot. Fry the spring rolls two at a time in the oil for 6–8 minutes. Make sure the fat is not too hot or the mixture inside will not heat through properly. Serve on a bed of salad leaves, mint, cilantro, and cucumber.

HOT AND SOUR CHICKEN SALAD

Ga Nuong Ngu Vi

This salad is also delicious with shrimp. Allow 1lb of fresh shrimp tails to serve 4.

SERVES 4–6

Ingredients
2 skinless chicken breasts
I small red chili, seeded and finely chopped
I piece fresh ginger, ½in long, peeled and finely chopped

I clove garlic, crushed
I tbsp crunchy peanut butter
2 tbsp chopped cilantro leaves
I tsp sugar
½ tsp salt
I tbsp rice or white wine vinegar
4 tbsp vegetable oil

2 tsp fish sauce (optional)
4oz bean sprouts
I head Napa cabbage, roughly shredded
2 medium carrots, cut into thin sticks
I red onion, cut into fine rings
2 large pickles, sliced

1 Slice the chicken thinly, place in a shallow bowl and set aside. Grind the chili, ginger, and garlic in a pestle and mortar. Add the peanut butter, cilantro, sugar, and salt.

2 Then add the vinegar, 2 tbsp of the oil and the fish sauce if using. Combine well. Cover the chicken with the spice mixture and leave to marinate for at least 2–3 hours.

3 Heat the remaining 2 tbsp of oil in a wok or frying pan. Add the chicken and cook for 10–12 minutes, tossing the meat occasionally. Serve arranged on the salad.

ALFALFA-CRAB SALAD WITH CRISPY FRIED NOODLES

Goi Gia

Alfalfa sprouts are available in many supermarkets. Alternatively, you can grow your own sprouts from seeds.

SERVES 4–6

Ingredients
vegetable oil, for deep-frying
2oz Chinese rice noodles, uncooked
2 dressed crabs, or 5oz frozen white crabmeat, thawed
4oz alfalfa sprouts

I small iceberg or bibb lettuce
4 sprigs cilantro, roughly chopped
I ripe tomato, skinned, seeded and diced
4 sprigs fresh mint, roughly chopped

Sesame lime dressing
3 tbsp vegetable oil
I tsp sesame oil

½ small red chili, seeded and finely chopped
I piece stem ginger in syrup, cut into matchsticks
2 tsp stem ginger syrup
2 tsp soy sauce
juice of ½ lime

1 Combine the vegetable and sesame oils in a bowl. Add the chili, stem ginger, stem ginger syrup, soy sauce and the lime juice.

2 Heat the oil in a deep-fryer to 385°F. Fry the noodles, one handful at a time, until crisp. Lift out and dry on paper.

3 Flake the white crabmeat into a bowl and toss with the alfalfa sprouts. Serve on a nest of noodles and tossed salad ingredients.

PORK BALLS WITH A MINTED PEANUT SAUCE

Nem Nuong

This recipe is equally delicious made with chicken breasts.

SERVES 4–6		**Minted peanut sauce**
Ingredients	1 egg white	2 tbsp smooth peanut butter
10oz leg of pork, trimmed and diced	½ tsp salt	juice of 1 lime
1 piece fresh ginger, ½in long, peeled and grated	a pinch of white pepper	1 red chili, seeded and finely chopped
1 clove garlic, crushed	12oz long-grain rice, washed and cooked for 15 minutes	1 clove garlic, crushed
2 tsp sesame oil	2oz ham, thickly sliced and diced	1 tbsp freshly chopped mint
1 tbsp medium-dry sherry	1 iceberg or bibb lettuce, to serve	1 tbsp freshly chopped cilantro
1 tbsp soy sauce		⅓ cup unsweetened cream of coconut
1 tsp sugar		1 tbsp fish sauce (optional)

1 To make the pork balls, place the diced pork, ginger, and garlic in a food processor and blend until smooth, about 2–3 minutes. Add the sesame oil, sherry, soy sauce, and sugar and blend. Add the egg white.

2 Spread the cooked rice and ham on a shallow dish. Using wet hands, shape the pork mixture into thumb-sized balls. Roll in the rice to cover and pierce each ball with a bamboo skewer.

3 To make the sauce, place the peanut butter in a bowl with the lime juice, chili, garlic, mint, and cilantro. Combine evenly, then add the cream of coconut and season with the fish sauce if using.

4 Place the pork balls in a bamboo steamer, cover, and steam over a saucepan of boiling water for 8–10 minutes. Arrange all the lettuce leaves on a large serving plate. Place the pork balls on the leaves with the dipping sauce on the side.

EXOTIC FRUIT SALAD

Hoa Qua Tron

A variety of fruits can be used for this salad depending on what is available. Look out for mandarin oranges, star fruit, paw paw, kiwi fruit, and passion fruit.

SERVES 4–6

Ingredients
6 tbsp sugar
1¼ cups water
2 tbsp stem ginger syrup
2 pieces star anise
1 piece cinnamon stick, 1 in long
1 clove
juice of ½ lemon
2 sprigs mint

1 medium pineapple
1 mango, peeled and sliced
2 bananas, sliced
8 lychees, fresh or canned
8oz fresh strawberries, trimmed and halved
2 pieces stem ginger, cut into sticks

1 Measure the sugar into a saucepan, and add the water, ginger syrup, spices, lemon juice, and mint. Bring to a boil and simmer for 3 minutes. Strain into a large bowl and allow to cool.

2 Remove both the top and bottom from the mango and remove the outer skin. Stand the mango on one end and remove the flesh in two pieces either side of the flat pit. Slice evenly and add to the syrup. Add the bananas, lychees, strawberries, and ginger. Chill until ready to serve.

3 Cut the pineapple in half down the centre. Loosen the flesh with a small serrated knife and remove to form two boat shapes. Cut the flesh into large chunks and place in the cooled syrup.

4 Spoon the fruit salad into the pineapple halves and bring to the table on a large serving dish. There will be enough fruit salad left over to refill the pineapple halves.

PORK AND NOODLE BROTH WITH SHRIMP

Pho

This quick and delicious recipe can be made with 7oz boneless chicken breast instead of pork tenderloin.

SERVES 4–6

Ingredients
12oz pork chops or 7oz pork tenderloin
8oz fresh shrimp tails or cooked shrimp
5oz thin egg noodles
1 tbsp vegetable oil
2 tsp sesame oil
4 shallots, or 1 medium onion, sliced
1 tbsp fresh ginger, finely sliced
1 clove garlic, crushed

1 tsp granulated sugar
6¼ cups chicken stock
2 lime leaves
3 tbsp fish sauce
juice of ½ lime
4 sprigs cilantro leaves, to garnish
chopped green part of 2 scallions, to garnish

1 If using pork chops, trim away fat and bone completely. Place the meat in the freezer for 30 minutes to firm but not freeze the meat. Slice the meat thinly and set aside. Peel and devein the shrimp, if fresh.

2 Bring a large saucepan of salted water to the boil and simmer the noodles for the time stated on the packet. Drain and refresh under cold running water. Set aside.

3 Heat the vegetable and sesame oils in a large saucepan, add the shallots, and brown evenly, for 3–4 minutes. Remove from the pan and set aside.

4 Add the ginger, garlic, sugar, and chicken stock and bring to a simmer with the lime leaves. Add the fish sauce and lime juice. Add the pork, then simmer for 15 minutes. Add the shrimp and noodles and simmer for 3–4 minutes. Serve in shallow soup bowls and decorate with the cilantro leaves, the green part of the scallions and the browned shallots.

VIETNAMESE DIPPING SAUCE

Nuoc Cham

Serve this dip in a small bowl as an accompaniment to spring rolls or meat dishes.

MAKES ⅔ CUP

Ingredients
1–2 small red chilies, seeded and finely chopped
1 clove garlic, crushed
1 tbsp roasted peanuts
4 tbsp coconut milk
2 tbsp fish sauce
juice of 1 lime
2 tsp sugar
1 tsp chopped cilantro leaves

---

1 Crush the red chili together with the garlic and peanuts using a pestle and mortar or food processor.

2 Add the coconut milk, fish sauce, lime juice, sugar, and cilantro.

HANDLING CHILIES

Chilies are an important part of Eastern cookery and should be handled with care. The pungent oils released when chilies are cut can be harmful to sensitive parts of the skin, especially to eyes and lips. Be sure to wash your hands thoroughly with soap and water after touching cut chilies.

1 The severe heat of red and green chilies is contained in the seeds. Unless you like fiercely hot food, the seeds should be discarded before using. It is most practical to wash the seeds away under cold running water.

2 A useful chili flavoring can be made by storing chilies in a jar of oil. Allow the hot flavors to merge for 3 weeks before using. Chili oil is used to add a gentle heat to many Eastern dishes.

CUCUMBER AND CARROT GARNISHES

Presentation is an important part of Southeast Asian cooking. These vegetable decorations are easily prepared.

MAKES 2 DECORATIVE GARNISHES

Ingredients
½ hothouse cucumber
1 large carrot

---

1 To make the cucumber garnish, cut the cucumber into a 3in strip, ¾in wide. Make 5 even cuts along the strip, ½in in from one end. Curl the second and fourth strips towards the base to form an open loop. The same cucumber strip can be spread out to form an attractive fan shape.

2 To make the carrot garnish, peel the carrot and cut into ¼in slices lengthways. Trim the slices into rectangles, ¾in × 3in. Make a ¼in cut along one edge of the carrot so that the strip is still joined. Make a second cut in the other direction, again so that the strip is joined. Bend the two ends together so that they cross over. This garnish can also be fashioned with giant white radish, cucumber, and lemon peel.

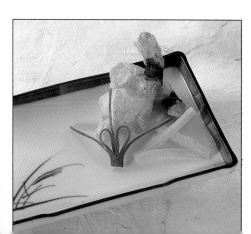

MAIN COURSE SPICY SHRIMP AND NOODLE SOUP

Laksa Lemak

This dish is served as a hot coconut broth with a separate platter of shrimp, fish, and noodles. Diners are invited to add their own choice of accompaniment to the broth.

SERVES 4–6

Ingredients

1oz raw cashew nuts
3 shallots, or 1 medium onion, sliced
1 piece lemongrass, 2in long, shredded
2 cloves garlic, crushed
2 tbsp vegetable oil
1 piece shrimp paste, ½in square, or
   1 tbsp fish sauce
1 tbsp mild curry paste
14oz canned coconut milk

½ chicken stock cube
3 curry leaves (optional)
1lb white fish fillet, cod, haddock, or whiting
8oz shrimp tails, fresh or cooked
1 small romaine lettuce, shredded
4oz bean sprouts
3 scallions, shredded
½ hothouse cucumber, sliced and shredded
5oz Laksa noodles (spaghetti-size rice noodles),
   soaked for 10 minutes before cooking
Shrimp Crackers, to serve

Cook's tip

To serve, line a large serving platter with the shredded lettuce leaves. Arrange the salad ingredients in neat piles together with the cooked fish, shrimp, and noodles. Serve the salad with a bowl of Shrimp Crackers and the broth in a lidded stoneware pot.

1 Grind the cashew nuts using a pestle and mortar or food processor with the shallots or onion, lemongrass and garlic. Cook the noodles according to the instructions.

2 Heat the oil in a large wok or saucepan, add the contents of the mortar or food processor, and fry until the nuts begin to brown, for about 1–2 minutes.

3 Add the shrimp paste or fish sauce and curry paste, followed by the coconut milk, stock cube, and curry leaves. Simmer for 10 minutes.

4 Cut the white fish into bite-size pieces. Place the fish and shrimp in a large frying basket, immerse into the simmering coconut stock, and cook for 3–4 minutes.

SESAME BAKED FISH WITH A HOT GINGER MARINADE

Panggang Bungkus

Tropical fish are found increasingly in supermarkets, but Asian markets usually have a wider selection.

SERVES 4–6

Ingredients

2 red snapper, parrot fish, or monkfish tails, weighing about 12oz each
2 tbsp vegetable oil
2 tsp sesame oil
2 tbsp sesame seeds
1 piece fresh ginger, 1in long, peeled and thinly sliced
2 cloves garlic, crushed

2 small red chilies, seeded and finely chopped
4 shallots or 1 medium onion, halved and sliced
2 tbsp water
1 piece shrimp paste, ½in square, or 1 tbsp fish sauce
2 tsp sugar
½ tsp cracked black pepper
juice of 2 limes
3–4 banana leaves, or aluminium foil
1 lime, to garnish
2 red chili flowers, to garnish

1 Clean the fish inside and out under cold running water. Pat dry with paper towels. Score both sides of each fish deeply with a knife to enable the marinade to penetrate effectively. If using parrot fish, rub with fine salt and leave to stand for 15 minutes. (This will remove the chalky coral flavor often associated with the parrot fish.)

2 To make the marinade, heat the vegetable and sesame oils in a wok, add the sesame seeds and fry until golden. Add the ginger, garlic, chilies and shallots or onion and soften over a gentle heat without burning. Add the water, shrimp paste or fish sauce, sugar, pepper, and lime juice, simmer for 2–3 minutes and allow to cool.

3 If using banana leaves, remove the central stem and discard. Soften the leaves by dipping in boiling water. To keep them supple, rub all over with vegetable oil. Spread the marinade over the fish, wrap in the banana leaf, and fasten with a bamboo skewer, or wrap the fish in foil. Leave the fish in a cool place to allow the flavors to mingle, for up to 3 hours.

4 Preheat the oven to 350°F or light a barbecue and allow the embers to settle to a steady glow. Place the wrapped fish on a wire rack or baking sheet and cook for between 35–40 minutes.

SPICY CLAY-POT CHICKEN

Ayam Golek

Clay-pot cooking stems from the practice of burying a glazed pot in the embers of an open fire. The gentle heat surrounds the base and keeps the liquid inside at a slow simmer, similar to the modern-day pot roast.

SERVES 4–6

Ingredients
1 × 3½lb chicken
3 tbsp freshly grated coconut
2 tbsp vegetable oil
2 shallots, or 1 small onion, finely chopped
2 cloves garlic, crushed

1 piece lemongrass, 2in long
1 piece galingal or fresh ginger, 1in long, peeled and thinly sliced
2 small green chilies, seeded and finely chopped
1 piece shrimp paste, ½in square, or 1 tbsp fish sauce
14fl oz canned coconut milk
1¼ cups chicken stock

2 lime leaves (optional)
1 tbsp sugar
1 tbsp rice or white wine vinegar
2 ripe tomatoes, to garnish
2 tbsp chopped cilantro leaves, to garnish
boiled rice, to serve

---

1 To joint the chicken, remove the legs and wings with a chopping knife. Skin the pieces and divide the drumsticks from the thighs and, using a pair of kitchen scissors, remove the lower part of the chicken leaving the breast piece. Remove as many of the bones as you can, to make the dish easier to eat. Cut the breast piece into 4 and set aside.

2 Dry-fry the coconut in a large wok until evenly brown. Add the vegetable oil, shallots or onion, garlic, lemongrass, galingal or ginger, chilies, and shrimp paste or fish sauce. Fry briefly to release the flavors. Preheat the oven to 350°F. Add the chicken joints to the wok and brown evenly with the spices for 2–3 minutes.

3 Strain the coconut milk, and add the thin part with the chicken stock, lime leaves if using, sugar, and vinegar. Transfer to a glazed clay pot, cover, and bake for 50–55 minutes or until the chicken is tender. Stir in the coconut milk solids and return to the oven for 5–10 minutes to simmer and thicken.

4 Place the tomatoes in a bowl and cover with boiling water to loosen and remove the skins. Halve the tomatoes, remove the seeds, and cut into large dice. Add the tomatoes to the finished dish, scatter with the chopped cilantro, and serve with a bowl of rice.

GREEN VEGETABLE SALAD WITH COCONUT MINT DIP

Syabas

This dish is served as an accompaniment to Singapore and Malaysian meat dishes.

SERVES 4–6

Ingredients
4oz snow peas, trimmed, stringed, and halved
4oz green beans, trimmed and halved
½ hothouse cucumber, halved and sliced
4oz Napa cabbage, roughly shredded

4oz bean sprouts
lettuce leaves, to serve

Dipping sauce
1 clove garlic, crushed
1 small green chili, seeded and finely chopped
2 tsp sugar

⅓ cup cream of coconut
2 tsp fish sauce
3 tbsp vegetable oil
juice of 1 lime
2 tbsp freshly chopped mint

1 Bring a saucepan of salted water to the boil. Blanch the snow peas, beans, and cucumber for 4 minutes. Refresh under cold running water. Drain and set aside.

2 To make the dressing, pound the garlic, chili and sugar together using a pestle and mortar. Add the cream of coconut, fish sauce, vegetable oil, lime juice, and mint.

3 Pour the dressing into a shallow bowl and serve with the salad ingredients arranged in an open basket.

SIZZLING STEAK

Daging

This method of sizzling meat on a hot grill can also be applied to sliced chicken or pork.

SERVES 4–6

Ingredients
4 × 7oz rump steaks
1 clove garlic, crushed
1 piece fresh ginger, 1 in long, peeled and finely chopped

2 tsp whole black peppercorns
1 tbsp sugar
2 tbsp tamarind sauce
3 tbsp dark soy sauce
1 tbsp oyster sauce
vegetable oil, for brushing

Dipping sauce
⅓ cup beef stock
2 tbsp tomato ketchup
1 tsp chili sauce
juice of 1 lime

1 Pound and blend all the ingredients together. Pour the marinade over the beef and allow the flavors to mingle for up to 8 hours.

2 Heat a cast-iron skillet over a high heat. Scrape the marinade from the meat and reserve. Brush the meat with oil and cook for 2 minutes on each side, or as you prefer.

3 Place the marinade in a pan, add the stock, sauces and lime juice, and simmer briefly. Serve the steaks and the dipping sauce separately.

CHICKEN SATAY WITH PEANUT SAUCE

Sate Ayam Saos Kacang

Both the marinated chicken and sauce can be stored in the freezer for up to 6 weeks. Allow 2 hours to thaw.

SERVES 4–6

Ingredients
4 boneless, skinless chicken breasts
1 tbsp coriander seeds
2 tsp fennel seeds
2 cloves garlic, crushed
1 piece lemongrass, 2in long, shredded
½ tsp turmeric
2 tsp sugar
½ tsp salt
2 tbsp soy sauce

1 tbsp sesame oil
juice of ½ lime
lettuce leaves, to serve
1 bunch mint leaves, to garnish
1 lime, quartered, to garnish
cucumber sticks, to garnish

Sauce
5oz raw peanuts
1 tbsp vegetable oil
2 shallots, or 1 small onion, finely chopped
1 clove garlic, crushed

1–2 small chilies, seeded and finely chopped
1 piece shrimp paste, ½in square, or 1 tbsp fish sauce
2 tbsp tamarind sauce
½ cup coconut milk
1 tbsp honey

1   Cut the chicken into long thin strips and thread, zig-zag, onto 12 bamboo skewers. Arrange on a flat plate and set aside.

2   To make the marinade, dry-fry the coriander and fennel seeds in a wok. Grind smoothly using a pestle and mortar or food processor, then add to the wok with the garlic, lemongrass, turmeric, sugar, salt, soy sauce, sesame oil, and lime juice. Allow the mixture to cool. Spread it over the chicken and leave in a cool place for up to 8 hours.

3   To make the peanut sauce, fry the peanuts in a wok with a little oil, or place under a moderate broiler, tossing them all the time to prevent burning. Transfer the peanuts to a clean cloth and rub vigorously with your hands to remove the papery skins. Place the peanuts in a food processor and blend for 2 minutes.

4   Heat the vegetable oil in a wok, and soften the shallots or onion, garlic, and chilies. Add the shrimp paste or fish sauce together with the tamarind sauce, coconut milk, and honey. Simmer briefly, add to the peanuts, and process to form a thick sauce. Heat the broiler to moderately hot. If using a barbecue, let the embers settle to a white glow. Brush the chicken with a little vegetable oil and cook for 6–8 minutes. Serve on a bed of lettuce, garnished, together with a bowl of dipping sauce.

HOT CHILI CRAB WITH GINGER AND LIME

Ikan Maris

Serve this dish with a bowl of cucumber sticks and hot slices of toast.

SERVES 4–6

Ingredients

2 medium crabs, cooked
1 piece fresh ginger, 1 in long, peeled and chopped
2 cloves garlic, crushed
1–2 small red chilies, seeded and finely chopped
1 tbsp sugar
2 tbsp vegetable oil
4 tbsp tomato ketchup
⅔ cup water
juice of 2 limes
2 tbsp freshly chopped cilantro leaves, to garnish

Cook's tip

Hot towels are useful towards the end of the meal to clean messy fingers. To prepare your own, moisten white cotton towels with cologne-scented water, wrap in a plastic bag, and microwave for 2 minutes at full power. Remove from the bag and bring to the table in a covered basket.

1 To prepare the crab, twist off the legs and claws. Crack open the thickest part of the shell with a hammer or the back of a knife.

2 Pry off the underside leg section with your two thumbs. From this section, remove the stomach sac and the grey gills, and discard. Cut the section into 4 with a knife. Cut the upper shell into 6 equal pieces.

3 Pound the ginger, garlic, chilies, and sugar using a pestle and mortar. Heat the vegetable oil in a large wok, add the pounded spices, and fry gently for about 1–2 minutes. Add the tomato ketchup, water, and lime juice and simmer briefly.

4 Add the pieces of crab and heat through for 3–4 minutes. Turn out into a serving bowl and scatter with the chopped cilantro.

MALAYSIAN FISH CURRY

Ikan Moolee

Hot Tomato Sambal is often served as an accompaniment to this dish.

SERVES 4–6

Ingredients
1 ½lb monkfish, hokey, or red snapper fillet
salt, to season
3 tbsp freshly grated or shredded coconut
2 tbsp vegetable oil
1 piece galingal or fresh ginger, 1in long, peeled

and thinly sliced
2 small red chilies, seeded and finely chopped
2 cloves garlic, crushed
1 piece lemongrass, 2in long, shredded
1 piece shrimp paste, ½in square, or 1 tbsp fish
  sauce
14oz canned coconut milk
2½ cups chicken stock

½ tsp turmeric
3 tsp sugar
juice of 1 lime, or ½ lemon

1 Cut the fish into large chunks, season with salt, and set aside.

2 Dry-fry the coconut in a large wok until evenly brown. Add the vegetable oil, galingal or ginger, chilies, garlic, and lemongrass and fry briefly. Stir in the shrimp paste or fish sauce. Strain the coconut milk, then add the thin coconut milk.

3 Add the chicken stock, turmeric, sugar, a little salt, and the lime or lemon juice. Simmer for 10 minutes. Add the fish and simmer for 6–8 minutes. Stir in the coconut milk solids, simmer gently to thicken, and serve with rice.

PLAIN BOILED RICE

A small amount of vegetable oil added to the rice will enhance its natural flavor.

SERVES 4–6

Ingredients
14oz long-grain rice
1 tbsp vegetable oil
3 cups boiling water
½ tsp salt

1 Wash and drain the rice several times in cold water until the water is no longer starchy. Put the rice in a heavy saucepan, add the vegetable oil, water, and salt. Stir once to prevent the rice from sticking to the pan and simmer for 10–12 minutes. After this time, remove from the heat, cover, and allow the rice to steam in its own heat for another 5 minutes. Fluff the rice with a fork or chopsticks before serving.

COCONUT RICE WITH LEMONGRASS

Serve this rice dish with Sizzling Steak or other meat dishes.

SERVES 4–6

Ingredients
14oz long-grain rice

½ tsp salt
1 piece lemongrass, 2in long
1oz unsweetened cream of coconut
3 cups boiling water

1 Wash and drain the rice several times in cold water until the water is no longer starchy. Put the rice, salt, lemongrass, and cream of coconut in a heavy saucepan, cover with the measured amount of boiling water. Stir once to prevent the grains from sticking, and simmer uncovered for 10–12 minutes.

2 Remove from the heat, cover, and allow to steam in its own heat for a further 5 minutes. Fluff the rice with a fork or chopsticks before serving.

SINGAPORE SLING

Singapore Sling is enjoyed in cocktail bars around the world. Recipes vary considerably, but they all use a standard measure that equates to a little less than 2 tbsp.

SERVES 1

Ingredients
ice
2 measures gin
1 measure cherry brandy
1 measure lemon juice
soda water, to taste
1 slice orange
1 slice lemon
1 Maraschino cherry, to garnish
1 mint sprig, to garnish

1 Wrap the ice in a clean cloth, and crush with a rolling pin or the underside of a saucepan. Half-fill a cocktail shaker with ice.

2 Add the gin, cherry brandy, and lemon juice and shake.

3 Strain the mixture into a goblet or tall glass over ice cubes. Fill with soda water to taste, and decorate with the slices of orange and lemon, and the cherry and mint.

SPECIAL FRIED NOODLES

Mee Goreng

Mee Goreng is perhaps the most well-known dish of Singapore. It is prepared from a wide range of ingredients.

SERVES 4–6

Ingredients
10oz egg noodles
1 skinless chicken breast
4oz lean pork
2 tbsp vegetable oil
6oz shrimp tails, fresh or cooked
4 shallots, or 1 medium onion, chopped
1 piece fresh ginger, ¾in long,
    peeled and thinly sliced
2 cloves garlic, crushed
3 tbsp light soy sauce
1–2 tsp chili sauce
1 tbsp rice or white-wine vinegar
1 tsp sugar
½ tsp salt
4oz Napa cabbage, shredded
4oz fresh spinach, shredded
3 scallions, shredded

1 Bring a large saucepan of salted water to the boil and cook the noodles according to the instructions on the packet. Drain and set aside. Place the chicken breast and pork in the freezer for 30 minutes to firm but not freeze.

2 Slice the meat thinly against the grain. Heat the oil in a large wok and fry the chicken, pork, and shrimp for 2–3 minutes. Add the shallots or onion, ginger, and garlic and fry without letting them color.

3 Add the soy and chili sauces, vinegar, sugar, and salt. Bring to a simmer, add the Napa cabbage, spinach, and scallions, cover, and cook for 3–4 minutes. Lastly add the noodles, heat through, and serve.

BROILED FISH WITH A CASHEW-GINGER MARINADE

Panggang Bungkus

To capture the sweet spicy flavors of this Indonesian favorite, marinated fish are wrapped in green banana leaves or foil and baked. The packets of fish are brought to the table, releasing a sweet spicy aroma.

SERVES 4

Ingredients

2½lb pomfret, parrot fish, or sea bass, scaled and cleaned
5oz raw cashew nuts
2 shallots, or 1 small onion, finely chopped
1 piece fresh ginger, ½in long, peeled and finely chopped
1 clove garlic, crushed

1 small red chili, seeded and finely chopped
2 tbsp vegetable oil
1 tbsp shrimp paste
2 tsp sugar
½ tsp salt
2 tbsp tamarind sauce
2 tbsp tomato ketchup
juice of 2 limes
4 young banana leaves, or aluminium foil

---

1 Score the fish 3–4 times on each side with a sharp knife to help it cook through to the bone. Set aside.

2 Grind the cashew nuts, shallots or onion, ginger, garlic, and chili to a fine paste using a pestle and mortar or food processor. Add the vegetable oil, shrimp paste, sugar, and salt and blend, then add the tamarind sauce, tomato ketchup, and lime juice.

Cook's tip

Banana leaves are readily available from Indian or Southeast Asian food stores. However, if these are difficult to obtain, simply wrap each fish in aluminium foil.

For an authentic taste of the Far East, the fish can be barbecued. Light the barbecue and allow the embers to settle to a steady glow. Cook each fish packet for 30–35 minutes.

3 Cover both sides of the fish with the marinade and leave for up to 8 hours to marinate.

4 To soften the banana leaves, remove the thick central stem and immerse the leaves in boiling water for 1 minute. Brush the leaves with vegetable oil. Wrap the fish in a banana leaf fastened with a bamboo skewer. Then preheat the oven to 350°F and bake for 30–35 minutes.

BEEF SATAY WITH A HOT MANGO DIP

Sate Bali

Serve this dish with a green salad and a bowl of plain rice.

MAKES 12 SKEWERS

Ingredients
1lb sirloin steak, ¾in thick, trimmed
1 tbsp coriander seeds
1 tsp cumin seeds
2oz raw cashew nuts
1 tbsp vegetable oil
2 shallots, or 1 small onion, finely chopped

1 piece fresh ginger, ½in long, peeled and finely chopped
1 clove garlic, crushed
2 tbsp tamarind sauce
2 tbsp dark soy sauce
2 tsp sugar
1 tsp rice or white-wine vinegar

Hot mango dip
1 ripe mango
1–2 small red chilies, seeded and finely chopped
1 tbsp fish sauce
juice of 1 lime
2 tsp sugar
¼ tsp salt
2 tbsp freshly chopped cilantro leaves

---

1 Slice the beef into long narrow strips and thread, zig-zag, onto 12 bamboo skewers. Lay on a flat plate and set aside.

2 For the marinade, dry-fry the seeds and nuts in a large wok until evenly brown. Place in a pestle and mortar with a rough surface and crush finely. Alternatively, blend the spices and nuts in a food processor. Add the vegetable oil, shallots or onion, ginger, garlic, tamarind and soy sauces, sugar, and vinegar. Spread this mixture over the beef and leave to marinate for up to 8 hours. Cook the beef under a moderate broiler or over a barbecue for 6–8 minutes, turning to ensure an even color. Meanwhile, make the mango dip.

3 Process the mango flesh with the chilies, fish sauce, lime juice, sugar, and salt until smooth, then add the cilantro.

SHRIMP SATAY WITH PAW PAW SAUCE

Udang Sate

Fresh shrimp are available frozen from reputable fishmongers. Chinese supermarkets also keep a good supply.

MAKES 12 SKEWERS

Ingredients
1½lb whole fresh shrimp tails or 24 jumbo shrimp
2 tbsp coriander seeds
2 tsp fennel seeds
2 shallots, or 1 small onion, finely chopped
1 piece fresh ginger, ½in long, peeled and finely chopped

2 cloves garlic, crushed
1 piece lemongrass, 2in long
2 tsp unsweetened cream of coconut
juice of 1 lime
1 tbsp fish sauce
2 tsp chili sauce
2 tbsp light soy sauce
4 tsp sugar
½ tsp salt

lettuce leaves, to serve

Sauce
2 ripe paw paws or papayas
juice of 1 lime
½ tsp freshly ground black pepper
pinch of salt
2 tbsp freshly chopped mint

---

1 Thread the shrimp onto 12 bamboo skewers and lay on a flat plate.

2 Dry-fry the coriander and fennel seeds, then pound smoothly in a pestle and mortar. Add the shallots or onion, ginger, garlic, and lemongrass and combine. Lastly add the cream of coconut, lime juice, fish, chili and soy sauces, sugar, and salt. Spread the sauce over the shrimp and leave in a cool place for up to 8 hours. Cook the shrimp under a moderate broiler or over a barbecue for 6–8 minutes, turning once.

3 Blend the paw paw, lime juice, pepper, and salt. Stir in the mint and serve.

SHRIMP CURRY WITH QUAILS' EGGS

Gulai Udang

Quails' eggs are available from speciality food shops and gourmet stores. Hens' eggs may be substituted if quails' eggs are hard to come by. Use 1 hen's egg to every 4 quails' eggs.

SERVES 4

Ingredients

2lb fresh shrimp tails, peeled and deveined
12 quails' eggs
2 tbsp vegetable oil
4 shallots or 1 medium onion, finely chopped
1 piece galingal or fresh ginger, 1in long, peeled and chopped
2 cloves garlic, crushed
1 piece lemongrass, 2in long, finely shredded
1–2 small red chilies, seeded and finely chopped
½ tsp turmeric
1 piece shrimp paste, ½in square, or 1 tbsp fish sauce
14fl oz canned coconut milk
1¼ cups chicken stock
4oz Napa cabbage, roughly shredded
2 tsp sugar
½ tsp salt
2 scallions, green part only, shredded, to garnish
2 tbsp shredded coconut, to garnish

1 Boil the quails' eggs for 8 minutes. Refresh in cold water, peel by dipping in cold water to release the shells, and set aside.

2 Heat the vegetable oil in a large wok, add the shallots or onion, galingal or ginger and garlic and soften without coloring. Add the lemongrass, chilies, turmeric, and shrimp paste or fish sauce and fry briefly to bring out their flavors.

3 Add the shrimp and fry briefly. Pour the coconut milk in a strainer over a bowl, then add the thin part of the milk with the chicken stock. Add the Napa cabbage, sugar, and salt and then bring to the boil. Simmer for 6–8 minutes.

4 Turn out onto a serving dish, halve the quails' eggs and toss in the sauce. Scatter with the scallions and the shredded coconut.

BROILED CASHEW NUT CHICKEN

Ayam Bali

This dish comes from the beautiful island of Bali where nuts are widely used as a base for sauces and marinades. Serve with a green salad and a hot chili dipping sauce such as Hot Chili and Garlic Dipping Sauce.

SERVES 4–6

Ingredients
4 chicken legs

Marinade
2oz raw cashew or macadamia nuts
2 shallots, or 1 small onion, finely chopped
2 cloves garlic, crushed
2 small red chilies, chopped
1 piece lemongrass, 2in long
1 tbsp tamarind sauce

2 tbsp dark soy sauce
1 tbsp fish sauce (optional)
2 tsp sugar
½ tsp salt
1 tbsp rice or white wine vinegar
Napa cabbage, to serve
radishes, sliced, to garnish
½ hothouse cucumber,
sliced, to garnish

1 Using a sharp knife, slash the chicken legs several times through to the bone, chop off the knuckle end, and set aside.

2 To make the marinade, place the cashew or macadamia nuts in a food processor or coarse pestle and mortar and grind.

3 Add the shallots or onion, garlic, chilies and lemongrass, and blend. Add the remaining marinade ingredients.

4 Spread the marinade over the chicken and leave in a cool place for up to 8 hours. Broil the chicken under a moderate heat or over a barbecue for 15 minutes on each side. Place on a dish lined with Napa cabbage and garnish with the sliced radishes and cucumber.

INDONESIAN PORK AND SHRIMP RICE

Nasi Goreng

Nasi Goreng is an attractive way of using up leftovers and appears in many variations throughout Indonesia. Rice is the main ingredient, although almost anything can be added for color and flavor.

SERVES 4–6

Ingredients
3 eggs
pinch of salt
4 tbsp vegetable oil
6 shallots, or 1 large onion, chopped
2 cloves garlic, crushed
1 piece fresh ginger, 1 in long, peeled and chopped

2–3 small red chilies, seeded and finely chopped
1 tbsp tamarind sauce
1 piece shrimp paste, ½in square, or 1 tbsp fish sauce
½ tsp turmeric
6 tsp unsweetened cream of coconut
juice of 2 limes
2 tsp sugar
½ tsp salt
12oz lean pork or chicken breasts,

skinned and sliced
12oz fresh or cooked shrimp tails, peeled
6oz bean sprouts
6oz Napa cabbage, shredded
6oz frozen peas, thawed
9oz long-grain rice, cooked to make 1½lb
1 small bunch cilantro or basil, roughly chopped, to garnish

1 In a bowl, beat the eggs with a pinch of salt. Heat a nonstick frying pan over a moderate heat. Pour in the eggs and move the pan around until they begin to set. When set, roll up, slice thinly, cover, and set aside.

2 Heat 1 tbsp of the oil in a wok and fry the shallots or onion until evenly brown. Remove from pan, set aside and keep warm.

3 Heat the remaining 3 tbsp of oil in the wok, add the garlic, ginger and chilies, and soften without coloring. Stir in the tamarind and shrimp paste or fish sauce, turmeric, cream of coconut, lime juice, sugar, and salt. Combine briefly over a moderate heat. Add the pork or chicken and shrimp, and fry for 3–4 minutes.

4 Toss the bean sprouts, Napa cabbage, and peas in the spices and cook briefly. Add the rice and stir-fry for 6–8 minutes, stirring to prevent it from burning. Transfer to a large serving plate, decorate with shredded egg pancake, the fried shallots or onion, and chopped cilantro or basil.

HOT TOMATO SAMBAL

Sambal Tomat

Sambals are placed on the table as a condiment and are used mainly for dipping meat and fish. They are very strong and should be used sparingly.

MAKES ½ CUP

Ingredients
3 ripe tomatoes, cored
½ tsp salt
I tsp chili sauce
4 tbsp fish sauce, or soy sauce
I tbsp chopped cilantro leaves

1 Cover the tomatoes with boiling water to loosen the skins. Remove the skins, halve, discard the seeds, and chop finely.

2 Place the chopped tomatoes in a bowl, add the salt, chili sauce, fish sauce or soy sauce, and cilantro.

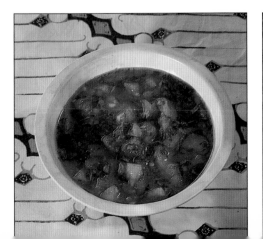

HOT CHILI AND GARLIC DIPPING SAUCE

Sambal Kecap

This sambal is particularly strong, so warn guests who are unaccustomed to spicy foods.

MAKES ½ CUP

Ingredients
I clove garlic, crushed
2 small red chilies, seeded and finely chopped
2 tsp sugar
I tsp tamarind sauce
4 tbsp soy sauce
juice of ½ lime

1 Pound the garlic, chilies, and sugar until smooth using a pestle and mortar, or grind in a food processor.

2 Add the tamarind sauce, soy sauce, and lime juice.

CUCUMBER SAMBAL

Sambal Selamat

This sambal has a piquant flavor without the hotness of chilies found in other recipes.

MAKES ⅔ CUP

Ingredients
I clove garlic, crushed
I tsp fennel seeds
2 tsp sugar
½ tsp salt
2 shallots, or I small onion, finely sliced
½ cup rice or white-wine vinegar
¼ hothouse cucumber, finely diced

1 Place the garlic, fennel seeds, sugar, and salt in a pestle and mortar and pound finely. Alternatively, grind the ingredients thoroughly in a food processor.

2 Stir in the shallots or onion, vinegar and cucumber and allow to stand for at least 6 hours to allow the flavors to combine.

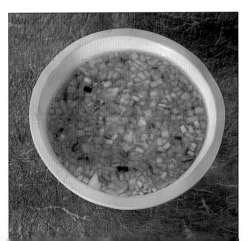

SPICY PEANUT RICE CAKES

Rempeyek

Serve these spicy rice cakes with a crisp green salad and a dipping sauce such as Hot Tomato Sambal.

MAKES 16 PIECES

Ingredients

1 clove garlic, crushed
1 piece fresh ginger, ½in long, peeled and finely chopped
¼ tsp turmeric
1 tsp sugar
½ tsp salt
1 tsp chili sauce
2 tsp fish or soy sauce

2 tbsp chopped cilantro leaves
juice of ½ lime
4oz long-grain rice, cooked
raw peanuts, chopped
¼ pint vegetable oil, for deep-frying

1 Pound together the garlic, ginger, and turmeric using a pestle and mortar. Add the sugar, salt, chili and fish or soy sauce, cilantro, and lime juice.

2 Add 3oz of the cooked rice and pound until smooth and sticky. Stir in the remainder of the rice. Wet your hands and shape into thumb-size balls.

3 Roll the balls in chopped peanuts to coat evenly. Then set aside until ready to cook and serve.

4 Heat the vegetable oil in a deep frying pan. Prepare a tray lined with paper towels to drain the rice cakes. Deep-fry 3 cakes at a time until crisp and golden, remove with a slotted spoon, then drain on paper towels.

VEGETABLE SALAD WITH A HOT PEANUT SAUCE

Gado Gado

Serve this vegetable salad with Indonesian Pork and Shrimp Rice and Shrimp Crackers. The peanut sauce is served separately from the salad, and everyone helps themselves.

SERVES 4–6

Ingredients
2 medium potatoes, peeled
6oz green beans, trimmed

Peanut sauce
5oz raw peanuts
1 tbsp vegetable oil
2 shallots, or 1 small onion, finely chopped

1 clove garlic, crushed
1–2 small chilies, seeded and finely chopped
1 piece shrimp paste, ½in square, or 1 tbsp fish sauce (optional)
2 tbsp tamarind sauce
½ cup canned coconut milk
1 tbsp clear honey

Salad ingredients
6oz Napa cabbage, shredded

1 iceberg or bibb lettuce
6oz bean sprouts
½ hothouse cucumber, cut into fingers
5oz giant white radish, shredded
3 scallions
8oz tofu, cut into large dice
3 hard-cooked eggs, quartered
1 small bunch cilantro

---

1 Bring the potatoes to the boil in salted water and simmer for 20 minutes. Cook the beans for 3–4 minutes. Drain the potatoes and beans and then refresh under cold running water.

2 For the peanut sauce, dry-fry the peanuts in a wok, or place under a moderate broiler, tossing them all the time to prevent burning. Transfer the peanuts to a clean cloth and rub vigorously with your hands to remove the papery skins. Place the peanuts in a food processor and blend for 2 minutes.

3 Heat the vegetable oil in a wok, and soften the shallots or onion, garlic, and chilies without letting them color. Add the shrimp paste or fish sauce if using, together with the tamarind sauce, coconut milk, and honey. Simmer briefly, add to the peanuts, and process to form a thick sauce.

4 Arrange the salad ingredients, potatoes, and beans on a large platter and serve with a bowl of the peanut sauce.

TABLE-TOP SIMMER POT

Ta Pin Lo

This meal is well-known in many Eastern countries and serves to unite all members of the family. The idea is to cook or reheat a range of ingredients displayed around a pot of simmering chicken stock. The meal is a great social occasion, and each person chooses their own selection of food. Dipping sauces are provided to season the dishes according to taste.

SERVES 4–6

Ingredients
6oz lean pork
6oz beef fillet
1 skinless chicken breast
8oz white fish fillets (monkfish, halibut, or hokey)
8oz tofu
16 fresh shrimp tails, peeled and deveined
7½ cups chicken stock
1 small red chili, split

1 piece fresh ginger, 1in long, peeled and sliced
6oz Chinese egg noodles, uncooked
8oz Napa cabbage, roughly shredded
1 iceberg, bibb, or romaine lettuce, shredded
6 scallions
½ hothouse cucumber, sliced
chili sauce
soy sauce
juice of 3 lemons

1 Place the pork, beef, and chicken in the freezer for 30 minutes to firm but not freeze. Slice the meat thinly and arrange on small side dishes.

2 Skin the fish and cut into thick chunks. Cut the tofu into large cubes and place it with the fish and shrimp tails on a small plate.

3 Bring the chicken stock to the boil with the chili and ginger in a saucepan or casserole that can be served at the table. A flame-lit fondue pot is ideal.

4 Simmer the noodles in a large pan of salted water according to the instructions on the packet. Refresh under cold running water, drain, and place in an attractive bowl.

5 Wash all the salad ingredients in water, drain, and arrange on separate plates.

6 Place the chili sauce, soy sauce, and lemon juice in three separate small dishes suitable for dipping and serve at the table. Fondue forks are ideal for dipping the meat and noodles, tofu, and fish into the stock, although in Singapore little wire baskets are used.

CHICKEN WONTON SOUP WITH SHRIMP

Ji Wun Tun Tang

This soup is a more luxurious version of basic Wonton Soup, and is almost a meal in itself.

SERVES 4	2 scallions, finely chopped	3¾ cups chicken stock
	1 egg	¼ hothouse cucumber, peeled and diced
Ingredients	2 tsp oyster sauce (optional)	1 scallion, roughly shredded, to garnish
11oz skinless chicken breast	salt and pepper	4 sprigs cilantro leaves, to garnish
7oz shrimp tails, fresh or cooked	1 packet wonton skins	1 tomato, skinned, seeded, and diced to garnish
1 tsp finely chopped fresh ginger	1 tbsp cornstarch paste	

1 Place the chicken breast, 5oz shrimp tails, ginger, and scallions in a food processor and mix for 2–3 minutes. Add the egg, oyster sauce, and seasoning and process briefly. Set to one side.

2 Place 8 wonton skins at a time on a surface, moisten the edges with cornstarch paste and place ½ tsp of the filling in the center of each. Fold in half and pinch to seal. Simmer in salted water for 4 minutes.

3 Bring the chicken stock to a boil, add the remaining shrimp tails, and the cucumber and simmer for 3–4 minutes. Add the wontons and simmer to warm through. Garnish and serve hot.

MALACCA FRIED RICE

Chow Fan

There are many versions of this dish throughout the East, all of which make use of leftover rice. Ingredients vary according to what is available, but shrimp are a popular addition.

SERVES 4–6	4 shallots or 1 medium onion, finely chopped	3 scallions, green part only, roughly chopped
	1 tsp finely chopped fresh ginger	8oz thickly sliced roast pork, diced
Ingredients	1 clove garlic, crushed	3 tbsp light soy sauce
2 eggs	8oz shrimp tails, fresh or cooked	12oz long-grain rice, cooked
salt and pepper	1–2 tsp chili sauce (optional)	
3 tbsp vegetable oil	8 oz frozen peas	

1 In a bowl, beat the eggs well and season. Heat 1 tbsp of the oil in a large nonstick frying pan, pour in the eggs, and allow to set without stirring for less than 1 minute. Roll up the pancake, cut into thin strips, and set aside.

2 Heat the remaining vegetable oil in a large wok, add the shallots, ginger, garlic, and shrimp tails and cook for 1–2 minutes; do not let the garlic burn.

3 Add the chili sauce, peas, scallions, pork, and soy sauce. Stir to heat through, then add the rice. Fry the rice over a moderate heat for 6–8 minutes. Transfer to a dish and decorate with the pancake.

PORK AND PEANUT WONTONS WITH PLUM SAUCE

Wanton Goreng

These crispy filled wontons are delicious served with Egg Pancake Salad Wrappers, a popular salad dish of Indonesia. The wontons can be filled and set aside for 8 hours before cooking.

MAKES 40–50 WONTONS

Ingredients
6oz ground pork or sausage meat
2 scallions, finely chopped
2 tbsp peanut butter
2 tsp oyster sauce (optional)
salt and pepper
1 packet wonton skins

2 tbsp flour paste
vegetable oil, for deep-frying

Plum Sauce
8oz dark plum jelly
1 tbsp rice or white-wine vinegar
1 tbsp dark soy sauce
½ tsp chili sauce

1 Combine the ground pork, scallions, peanut butter, oyster sauce, and seasoning and set aside.

2 For the plum sauce, combine the plum jelly, vinegar, soy and chili sauces in a serving bowl and set aside.

3 To fill the wonton skins, place 8 wrappers at a time on a work surface, moisten the edges with the flour paste, and place ½ tsp of the pork mixture on each one. Fold in half, corner to corner, and twist.

4 Fill a wok or deep frying pan one-third with vegetable oil and heat to 385°F. Have a wire strainer or frying basket ready and a tray lined with paper towels. Drop the wontons, 8 at a time, in the hot fat and fry until golden, for about 1–2 minutes. Lift out onto the paper-lined tray and sprinkle with fine salt. Place the plum sauce on a serving plate and surround with the crispy wontons.

HOT CHILI SHRIMP

Udang

Hot Chili Prawns can be prepared about 8 hours in advance and are best broiled or barbecued.

SERVES 4–6

Ingredients
1 clove garlic, crushed
1 piece fresh ginger, ½in long, peeled and chopped
1 small red chili, seeded and chopped
2 tsp sugar
1 tbsp light soy sauce
1 tbsp vegetable oil
1 tsp sesame oil
juice of 1 lime
salt, to taste
1½lb whole shrimp, uncooked
6oz cherry tomatoes
½ hothouse cucumber, cut into chunks
1 small bunch cilantro, roughly chopped

---

1 Pound the garlic, ginger, chili, and sugar to a paste using a pestle and mortar. Add the soy sauce, vegetable and sesame oils, lime juice, and salt. Cover the shrimp with the marinade and allow to marinate for as long as possible, preferable 8 hours.

2 Thread the shrimp, tomatoes, and cucumber onto bamboo skewers. Broil the shrimp for 3–4 minutes, scatter with the cilantro, and serve.

SHRIMP CRACKERS

Krupuk

Shrimp Crackers are a popular addition to many Far Eastern dishes and are often served before guests come to the table. Some supermarkets and food stores sell crackers ready for cooking.

SERVES 4–6

Ingredients
1¼ cups vegetable oil
2oz uncooked shrimp crackers
fine table salt, to taste

---

1 Line a tray with paper towels. Heat the oil in a large wok until it begins to smoke. Lower the heat to maintain a steady temperature.

2 Drop 3–4 prawn crackers into the oil. Remove from the oil before they begin to color and transfer to the paper-lined tray. Serve sprinkled with salt.

SWEET AND SOUR GINGER SAMBAL

Sambal Jahe

Sambals are a common sight at Indonesian and Malaysian tables. Their purpose is to perk-up or cool down hot chili flavors. Sambals can also include simple components such as onion and cucumber.

MAKES 6 TBSP

Ingredients
4–5 small red chilis, seeded and chopped
2 shallots, or 1 small onion, chopped
2 cloves garlic
1 piece fresh ginger, ¾in long, peeled
2 tbsp sugar
¼ tsp salt
3 tbsp rice or white-wine vinegar

---

1 Finely pound or grind the chilies and shallots or onion together using a pestle and mortar or food processor.

2 Add the garlic, ginger, sugar, and salt and continue to grind until smooth. Lastly add the vinegar, combine, and pour into an airtight container.

SPICY PORK WITH LEMONGRASS AND COCONUT

Semur Daging

Serve this dish with plain boiled rice and Hot Tomato Sambal.

SERVES 4–6	4 shallots, or 1 medium onion, chopped	1¼ cups chicken stock
	1 piece lemongrass, 2in long, finely shredded	1 tsp sugar
Ingredients	1–2 small red chilies, seeded and finely chopped	juice of 1 lemon
1½lb lean pork	1 piece shrimp paste, ½in square	zest of 1 satsuma, finely shredded
2 tbsp vegetable oil	14oz canned coconut milk	1 small bunch cilantro, chopped

3 Add the coconut milk, chicken stock, sugar, and lemon juice. Return to a boil and simmer for 15–20 minutes. Transfer the pork to a serving dish and sprinkle with the zest of the satsuma and the cilantro.

1 Place the pork in the freezer for 30 minutes. Slice the meat thinly.

2 Heat the vegetable oil in a large wok, add the shallots or onion, lemongrass, chilies, and shrimp paste. Add the pork and seal.

EGG PANCAKE SALAD WRAPPERS

Nonya Popiah

One of Indonesia's favorite snack foods, pancakes are assembled according to taste and dipped in various sauces.

SERVES 4–6	1 iceberg or bibb lettuce	1 small red chili, seeded and finely chopped
	4oz bean sprouts	1 tbsp rice or white-wine vinegar
Ingredients		2 tsp sugar
2 eggs	**Filling**	4oz giant white radish, peeled and grated
½ tsp salt	3 tbsp vegetable oil	1 medium carrot, grated
1 tsp vegetable oil, plus a little for frying	1 piece fresh ginger, ½in long, peeled and	4oz Napa or white cabbage, shredded
1 cup all-purpose flour	chopped	2 shallots or 1 small red onion, thinly sliced
1¼ cups water	1 clive garlic, crushed	

1 Break the eggs into a bowl, add the salt, vegetable oil, and flour and stir until smooth. Do not overmix. Add the water, a little at a time, and strain into a jug. Allow the batter to stand for 15–20 minutes.

2 Moisten a small nonstick frying pan with vegetable oil and heat. Cover the base of the pan with batter and cook for 30 seconds. Turn over and cook briefly. Stack the pancakes on a plate, cover, and keep warm.

3 Heat the oil in a large work, add the ginger, garlic, and chili and fry gently. Add the vinegar, sugar, white radish, carrot, cabbage, and shallots. Cook for 3–4 minutes. Serve with the pancakes and salad.

PHILIPPINES

FILIPINO CHICKEN POT

Puchero

This nourishing main course soup is one of many brought to the Philippines by the Spanish in the sixteenth century. The recipe and method are based on Potajes, a special stew still enjoyed throughout much of Spain. In the Philippines, ingredients vary according to what is available, but the dish still retains much of its original character.

SERVES 4–6

Ingredients
6oz dried white beans
3 chicken legs
1 tbsp vegetable oil
12oz lean pork, diced
1 chorizo (optional)
1 small carrot, peeled and roughly chopped
1 medium onion, roughly chopped
7½ cups water
1 clove garlic, crushed

2 tbsp tomato paste
1 bay leaf
2 chicken stock cubes
12oz sweet potatoes or new potatoes, peeled
2 tsp chili sauce
2 tbsp white-wine vinegar
3 firm tomatoes, skinned, seeded, and chopped
8oz Napa cabbage
salt and freshly ground black pepper
3 scallions, shredded
boiled rice, to serve

1 Soak the beans in plenty of cold water for 8 hours. Drain.

2 Divide the chicken drumsticks from the thighs. Chop off the narrow end of each drumstick and discard.

3 Heat the vegetable oil in a wok or large saucepan, add the chicken, pork, sliced chorizo if using, carrot, and onion, then brown.

4 Drain the white beans, and add with the water, garlic, tomato paste, and bay leaf. Bring to a boil and simmer for 2 hours until the beans are almost tender.

5 Crumble in the chicken stock cubes, add the sweet or new potatoes, and the chili sauce, then simmer for 15–20 minutes until the potatoes are cooked.

6 Add the vinegar, tomatoes, and Napa cabbage, then simmer for 1–2 minutes. Season to taste with salt and pepper. The *Puchero* is intended to provide enough liquid to be served as a first course broth. This is followed by a main course of the meat and vegetables scattered with the shredded scallions. Serve with rice as an accompaniment.

SWEET AND SOUR PORK WITH COCONUT SAUCE

Adobo

Adobo is a popular dish of the Philippines. Typically the meat is tenderized in a marinade before being cooked in coconut milk, shallow-fried, and returned to the sauce. Beef, chicken, and fish Adobos are also popular.

SERVES 4–6	1 tbsp sugar	and roughly chopped
	⅔ cup palm or cider vinegar	salt
Ingredients	2 small bay leaves	½ hothouse cucumber, peeled and cut into sticks
1½lb lean pork, diced	1¼ cups chicken stock	2 firm tomatoes, peeled, seeded, and chopped
1 clove garlic, crushed	2oz unsweetened cream of coconut	1 small bunch chives, chopped
1 tsp paprika	⅔ cup vegetable oil or shortening, for frying	
1 tsp cracked black pepper	1 under-ripe papaya or paw paw, peeled, seeded,	

1 Marinate the pork, garlic, paprika, black pepper, sugar, vinegar, and bay leaves for 2 hours. Add the stock and coconut.

2 Simmer gently for 30–35 minutes, remove pork, and drain. Heat the oil and brown the pork evenly. Remove and drain.

3 Return the pork to the sauce with the papaya or paw paw, season, and simmer for 15–20 minutes. Add garnishes and serve.

NOODLES WITH CHICKEN, SHRIMP, AND HAM

Pansit Guisado

Egg noodles can be cooked up to 24 hours in advance and kept in a bowl of cold water.

SERVES 4–6	2oz canned water chestnuts, sliced	7oz canned baby corn, drained
	1 tbsp light soy sauce	2 limes, cut into wedges, to garnish
Ingredients	2 tbsp fish sauce, or strong chicken stock	1 small bunch cilantro, shredded, to garnish
10oz dried egg noodles	6oz cooked chicken breast, sliced	
1 tbsp vegetable oil	5oz cooked ham, thickly sliced, cut into	
1 medium onion, chopped	short fingers	
1 clove garlic, crushed	8oz shrimp tails, cooked and peeled	
1 piece fresh ginger, peeled and chopped	6oz bean sprouts	

1 Cook the noodles according to the packet. Drain and set aside.

2 Fry the onion, garlic, and ginger until soft. Add the chestnuts, sauces, and meat.

3 Add the noodles, bean sprouts, and corn. Stir-fry for 6–8 minutes.

BRAISED BEEF IN A RICH PEANUT SAUCE

Kari Kari

Like many dishes brought to the Philippines by the Spanish, this slow-cooking Estofado, renamed Kari Kari, retains much of its original charm. Rice and peanuts are used to thicken the juices, yielding a rich glossy sauce.

SERVES 4–6

Ingredients
2lb stewing beef (chuck is best)
2 tbsp vegetable oil
1 tbsp annatto seeds, or 1 tsp paprika and a pinch of turmeric
2 medium onions, chopped
2 cloves garlic, crushed
10oz celeriac or rutabaga, peeled and roughly chopped
1¾ cups beef stock
12oz new potatoes, peeled and cut into large dice
1 tbsp fish or anchovy sauce
2 tbsp tamarind sauce
2 tsp sugar
1 bay leaf
1 sprig thyme
3 tbsp long-grain rice, soaked in water
2oz peanuts or 2 tbsp peanut butter
1 tbsp white-wine vinegar
salt and freshly ground black pepper, to taste

1   Cut the beef into 1in cubes and set aside. Heat the vegetable oil in a flame-proof casserole, add the annatto seeds if using, and stir to color the oil dark red. Remove the seeds with a slotted spoon and discard. If you are not using annatto seeds, paprika and turmeric can be added later.

2   Soften the onions, garlic, and the celeriac or rutabaga in the oil without letting them color. Add the beef and sear to keep in the flavor. If you are not using annatto seeds to redden the sauce, stir the paprika and turmeric in with the beef. Add the beef stock, potatoes, fish or anchovy and tamarind sauces, sugar, bay leaf, and thyme. Bring to a simmer and allow to cook on top of the stove for 2 hours.

3   Cover the rice with cold water and leave to stand for 30 minutes. Roast the peanuts under a hot broiler, if using, then rub the skins off in a clean cloth. Drain the rice and grind with the peanuts or peanut butter using a pestle and mortar, or food processor.

4   When the beef is tender, add 4 tbsp of the cooking liquid to the ground rice and nuts. Blend smoothly and stir into the stew. Simmer gently on the stove to thicken, for about 15–20 minutes. To finish, stir in the wine vinegar and season well with the salt and freshly ground pepper.

SUGAR BREAD ROLLS

Ensaimadas

In the Philippines, pots of coffee and hot milky chocolate are brought out for a special custom called the merienda. Meriendas occur morning and afternoon and call for a lavish display of cakes and breads. Many are flavored with sweet coconut although these delicious rolls of Spanish origin are enriched with butter, eggs, and cheese.

MAKES 10 ROLLS

Ingredients
2⅔ cups white bread flour
1 tsp salt
1 tbsp superfine sugar
⅔ cup lukewarm water

1 tsp dried yeast
3 egg yolks
3 tbsp sweet butter, softened
3oz Cheddar cheese, grated
6 tsp sweet butter, melted
6 tbsp sugar

1 Sift the flour, salt, and superfine sugar into a food processor fitted with a dough blade or an electric mixer fitted with a dough hook, then make a well in the center. Dissolve the yeast in the lukewarm water and pour into the well. Add the egg yolks and leave for a few minutes until bubbles appear on the surface of the liquid.

2 Combine the ingredients for less than 1 minute into a firm dough. Add the 2oz of butter and knead until smooth, for about 2–3 minutes, or 4–5 minutes if using an electric mixer. Transfer the dough to a floured bowl, cover, and leave to rise in a warm place until it doubles in volume.

3 Preheat the oven to 375°F. Transfer the dough to a lightly floured work surface and divide into 10 pieces. Spread the grated cheese over the surface and roll each of the pieces into 5in lengths. Coil into snail shapes and place on a lightly greased, high-sided tray or pan measuring 12 × 8in.

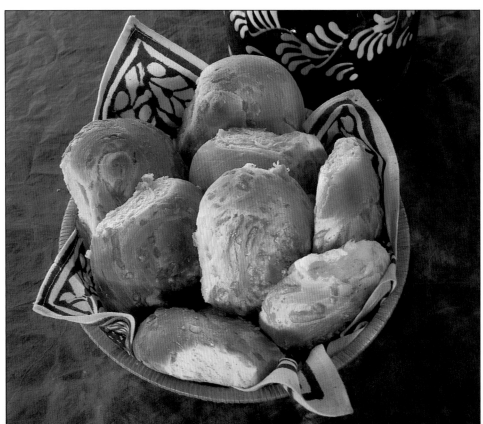

4 Cover the tray with a loose-fitting plastic bag and leave to rise for a second time until the dough doubles in volume, for about 45 minutes, or up to 2 hours if conditions are not warm. Bake for 20–25 minutes. Brush with the melted butter, sprinkle with the sugar and allow to cool. Break up the rolls and serve in a lined basket.

SWEET AND SOUR PORK AND SHRIMP SOUP

Sinegang

This main course soup has a sour, rich flavor. Under-ripe fruits and vegetables provide a special tartness.

SERVES 4–6		
Ingredients	1 small, under-ripe mango, peeled, flesh removed, and chopped	1 star fruit, thickly sliced
12oz lean pork, diced	6¼ cups chicken stock	3oz green cabbage, shredded
8oz raw or cooked shrimp tails, peeled	1 tbsp fish or soy sauce	salt
2 tbsp tamarind sauce	10oz sweet potato, peeled and cut into even pieces	1 tsp crushed black pepper
juice of 2 limes	8oz unripe tomatoes, quartered	2 scallions, shredded, to garnish
1 small green guava, peeled, halved, and seeded	4oz green beans, trimmed and halved	2 limes, quartered, to garnish

1 Trim the pork, peel the shrimp, and set aside. Measure the tamarind sauce and lime juice into a saucepan.

2 Add the pork, guava, and mango. Pour in the stock. Add the fish or soy sauce and simmer, uncovered, for 30 minutes.

3 Add the remaining fruit, vegetables, and shrimp. Simmer for 10–15 minutes. Adjust seasoning, garnish, and serve.

SAVORY PORK PIES

Empanadas

These are native to Galicia in Spain and were brought to the Philippines in the sixteenth century.

MAKES 12 PASTRIES
Ingredients
12oz frozen pastry, thawed
Filling
1 tbsp vegetable oil
1 medium onion, chopped
1 clove garlic, crushed
1 tsp thyme
4oz ground pork
1 tsp paprika
salt and freshly ground black pepper
1 hard cooked egg, chopped
1 medium pickle, chopped
2 tbsp freshly chopped parsley
vegetable oil, for deep-frying

1 To make the filling, heat the vegetable oil in a frying pan or wok and soften the onions, garlic, and thyme without browning, for about 3–4 minutes. Add the pork and paprika, then brown evenly for 6–8 minutes. Season well, transfer to a bowl and cool. When the mixture is cool, add the hard cooked egg, pickle, and parsley.

2 Transfer the pastry to a floured work surface and roll out to a 15in square. Cut out 12 circles 5in in diameter. Place 1 tbsp of the filling on each circle, moisten the edges with a little water, fold over, and seal. Heat the vegetable oil in a deep-fryer, fitted with a basket, to 385°F. Place 3 Empanadas at a time in the basket and deep-fry until golden brown. Frying should take at least 1 minute or the inside filling will not be heated through. Serve warm in a basket covered with a napkin.

SWEET POTATO AND PUMPKIN SHRIMP CAKES

Ukoy

These delicious fried cakes should be served warm with a fish sauce or a dark soy sauce.

SERVES 4–6

Ingredients

7oz fresh shrimp tails, peeled and
   roughly chopped
7oz white bread flour
½ tsp salt

½ tsp dried yeast
¾ cup lukewarm water
1 egg, beaten
5oz sweet potato, peeled and grated
8oz pumpkin, peeled, seeded, and grated
2 scallions, chopped
2oz water chestnuts, sliced and chopped

½ tsp chili sauce
1 clove garlic, crushed
juice of ½ lime
vegetable oil, for deep-frying

---

1 Sift the flour and salt into a mixing bowl and make a well in the center. Dissolve the yeast in the water, then pour into the well. Pour in the egg and leave for a few minutes until bubbles appear. Mix to a batter.

2 Place the peeled shrimp in a saucepan and cover with water. Bring to a boil and simmer for 10–12 minutes. Drain and refresh in cold water. Roughly chop and set aside. Add the sweet potato and pumpkin.

3 Then add the scallions, water chestnuts, chili sauce, garlic, lime juice, and shrimp. Heat a little oil in a large frying pan. Spoon in the batter in small heaps and fry until golden. Drain and serve.

FILIPINO HOT CHOCOLATE

Napalet a Chocolate

This luxurious hot chocolate is served for merienda with Sugar Bread Rolls or Coconut Rice Fritters.

SERVES 2

Ingredients
2 tbsp sugar
½ cup water
4oz best-quality semi-sweet chocolate
scant 1 cup evaporated milk

1 Measure the sugar and water into a nonstick saucepan. Simmer to make a basic syrup.

2 Break the chocolate into even pieces, add to the syrup, and stir until melted.

3 Add the evaporated milk, return to a simmer, and whisk to a froth. Divide between 2 tall mugs and serve.

COCONUT RICE FRITTERS

Puto

These delicious fritters can be served any time, with a mug of steaming coffee or chocolate.

MAKES 28 FRITTERS

Ingredients
5oz long-grain rice, cooked
2 tbsp coconut milk powder
3 tbsp sugar
2 egg yolks
juice of ½ lemon
3oz shredded coconut
oil, for deep-frying
confectioners' sugar, for dusting

1 Place 3oz of the cooked rice in a pestle and mortar and pound until smooth and sticky. Alternatively, use a food processor. Transfer to a large bowl, combine with the remainder of the rice, the coconut milk powder, sugar, egg yolks, and lemon juice. Spread the shredded coconut onto a tray, divide the mixture into thumb-size pieces with wet hands, and then roll in the coconut into neat balls.

2 Heat a wok or deep-fat fryer fitted with a wire basket to 350°F. Fry the coconut rice balls, 3–4 at a time, for 1–2 minutes until the coconut is evenly brown. Transfer to a plate, and dust with confectioners' sugar. Place a wooden skewer in each fritter and serve with café au lait or hot chocolate at merienda time.

BEEF AND VEGETABLES IN A TABLE-TOP BROTH

Shabu Shabu

Shabu Shabu is the perfect introduction to Japanese cooking and is well suited to party gatherings. The name refers to the swishing sound made as wafer-thin slices of beef, tofu, and vegetables cook in a special broth.

SERVES 4–6

Ingredients
1 lb beef sirloin, trimmed
7½ cups water
½ sachet of instant Dashi powder, or ½ vegetable stock cube
5oz carrots
6 scallions, trimmed and sliced
5oz Napa cabbage, roughly shredded
8oz giant white radish, peeled and shredded

10oz Udon, or fine wheat noodles, cooked
4oz canned bamboo shoots, sliced
6oz tofu, cut into large dice
10 shiitake mushrooms, fresh or dried

Sesame dipping sauce
2oz sesame seeds, or 2 tbsp tahini paste
½ cup instant Dashi stock, or vegetable stock
4 tbsp dark soy sauce
2 tsp sugar

2 tbsp sake (optional)
2 tsp Wasabi powder (optional)

Ponzu dipping sauce
⅓ cup lemon juice
1 tbsp rice or white-wine vinegar
⅓ cup dark soy sauce
1 tbsp Tamari sauce
1 tbsp Mirin, or 1 tsp sugar
¼ tsp instant Dashi powder, or ¼ vegetable stock cube

---

1 Place the meat in the freezer for 30 minutes until firm but not frozen. Slice the meat with a large knife or cleaver. Arrange neatly on a plate, cover, and set aside. Bring the water to a boil in a Japanese donabe, or any other covered flame-proof casserole that is unglazed on the outside. Stir in the Dashi powder or stock cube, cover, and simmer for 8–10 minutes. Serve at the table standing on its own heat source.

2 To prepare the vegetables, bring a saucepan of salted water to the boil. Peel the carrots and with a canelle knife cut a series of grooves along their length. Slice the carrots thinly and blanch for 2–3 minutes. Blanch the scallions, Napa cabbage, and giant white radish for the same time. Arrange the vegetables with the noodles, bamboo shoots, and tofu. Slice the mushrooms (soak dried mushrooms in boiling water for 3–4 minutes).

3 To make the sesame dipping sauce, dry-fry the sesame seeds, if using, in a heavy frying pan, taking care not to burn them. Grind the seeds smoothly using a pestle and mortar with a rough surface. Alternatively, you can use tahini paste.

4 Add the remaining ingredients, combine well, then pour into a shallow dish. Sesame dipping sauce will keep in the refrigerator for 3–4 days.

5 To make the Ponzu dipping sauce, put the ingredients into a screw-top jar and shake well. Provide guests with chopsticks and individual bowls, so they can help themselves to what they want. Towards the end of the meal, each guest takes a portion of noodles and ladles the well-flavored stock over them.

Cook's tip

Dashi is the name given to Japan's most common stock. The flavour derives from a special seaweed known as kelp. This light-tasting stock is available in powder form from oriental food stores. Diluted vegetable stock cube is a good substitute for Dashi.

Tahini paste is a purée of toasted sesame seeds that is used mainly in Middle Eastern cooking. It is available in large supermarkets and specialist food shops.

MISO BREAKFAST SOUP

Miso-shiru

Miso is a fermented bean paste that adds richness and flavor to many of Japan's favorite soups. This soup provides a nourishing start to the day. Miso paste is widely available in health food stores.

MAKES 5 CUPS	5 cups Dashi, or light vegetable stock
	4 tbsp Miso
Ingredients	4oz tofu, cut into large dice
3 shiitake mushrooms, fresh or dried	I scallion, green part only, sliced

1 Slice the mushrooms thinly. If they are dried, soak them first in boiling water for 3–4 minutes. Set aside.

2 Bring the Dashi or light vegetable stock to a boil. Stir in the Miso, add the mushrooms, and simmer for 5 minutes.

3 Ladle the broth into 4 soup bowls and place the tofu in each. Add the scallion and serve.

CRAB AND TOFU DUMPLINGS

Kami-dofu Iridashi

These little crab and ginger dumplings are served as a delicious side accompaniment.

MAKES 30	¼ tsp salt	**Dipping sauce**
	2 tsp light soy sauce	½ cup Dashi, or light vegetable
Ingredients	2 tbsp scallion, green part only, finely chopped	stock
4oz frozen white crabmeat, thawed	I piece fresh ginger, ¾in long, peeled and grated	3 tbsp Mirin, or I tbsp sugar
4oz tofu, drained	vegetable oil, for deep-frying	3 tbsp dark soy sauce
I egg yolk	2oz giant white radish, finely grated	
2 tbsp rice flour, or wheat flour		

1 Squeeze as much moisture out of the crabmeat as you can before using. Press the tofu through a fine strainer with the back of a spoon and then combine with the crabmeat in a bowl.

2 Add the egg yolk, rice flour, salt, scallion, ginger, and soy sauce to the tofu and crabmeat and stir to form a light paste. Set aside. To prepare the dipping sauce, combine the Dashi or stock with the Mirin or sugar and soy sauce.

3 Line a tray with paper towels. Heat the vegetable oil to 385°F. Shape the mixture to make thumb-size pieces. Fry 6 at a time for 1–2 minutes. Drain on the paper. Serve with the sauce and radish.

BARBECUE-GLAZED CHICKEN SKEWERS

Yakitori

Yakitori is popular throughout Japan and is often served as an appetizer with drinks.

MAKES 12 SKEWERS AND 8 WING PIECES

Ingredients
4 chicken thighs, skinned
4 scallions, blanched and cut into short lengths
8 chicken wings

Basting sauce
4 tbsp sake
⅓ cup dark soy sauce
2 tbsp Tamari sauce
3 tbsp Mirin, or sweet sherry
4 tbsp sugar

1 Bone the chicken thighs and cut the meat into large dice. Thread the scallions and chicken onto 12 skewers.

2 To prepare the chicken wings, remove the wing tip at the first joint. Chop through the second joint, revealing the two narrow bones. Take hold of the bones with a clean cloth and pull, turning the meat around the bones inside out. Remove the smaller bone and set aside.

3 Measure the basting sauce ingredients into a stainless steel or enamel saucepan and simmer until reduced by two-thirds. Cool. Heat the broiler to a moderately high temperature. Broil the skewers without applying any oil. When juices begin to emerge from the chicken, baste liberally with the basting sauce. Allow 3 minutes more for the chicken on skewers and not more than 5 minutes for the wings.

RAW FISH AND RICE PARCELS

Sushi

Sushi is something of an art form in Japan, but with a little practice it is possible to make sushi at home.

MAKES 8–10

Ingredients

Tuna sushi
3 sheets nori (paper-thin seaweed)
5oz freshest tuna fillet, cut into fingers
1 tsp Wasabi, made into a thin paste
    with a little water
6 young carrots, blanched
1lb cooked sushi rice

Salmon sushi
2 eggs
½ tsp salt
2 tsp sugar
5 sheets nori
1lb cooked sushi rice
5oz freshest salmon fillet, cut into fingers
1 tsp Wasabi, made into a thin paste
    with a little water
½ small cucumber, cut into strips

1 To make the tuna sushi, spread half a sheet of nori onto a bamboo mat, lay strips of tuna across the full length and season with the thinned Wasabi. Place a line of blanched carrot next to the tuna and roll tightly. Moisten the edge with water and seal. Place a square of damp wax paper onto the bamboo mat, then spread evenly with sushi rice. Place the seaweed-wrapped tuna along the center and wrap tightly, enclosing the seaweed completely. Remove the paper and cut into neat rounds with a wet knife.

2 To make the salmon sushi, make a simple flat omelete by beating together the eggs, salt and sugar. Heat a large nonstick pan, pour in the egg mixture, stir briefly, and allow to set. Transfer to a clean cloth and cool. Place the nori onto a bamboo mat, cover with the omelete, and trim to size. Spread a layer of rice over the omelete then lay strips of salmon across the width. Season the salmon with the thinned Wasabi, then place a strip of cucumber next to the salmon. Fold the bamboo mat in half, forming a tear shape inside. Cut into neat sections with a wet knife.

SALT-BROILED MACKEREL

Shio-yaki

Shio-yaki means salt-broiled. In Japan, salt is applied to oily fish before cooking to draw out the flavors. Mackerel, garfish, and snapper are the most popular choices, all of which develop a unique flavor and texture when treated with salt. The salt is washed away before cooking.

SERVES 2	Soy-ginger dip	Japanese horseradish
Ingredients	4 tbsp dark soy sauce	3 tsp Wasabi powder
2 small or 1 large mackerel, snapper, or garfish, gutted and cleaned, with head on	2 tbsp sugar	2 tsp water
	1 piece fresh ginger, 1 in long, peeled and finely grated	1 medium carrot, peeled and shredded
2 tbsp fine sea salt		

1 Rinse the fish under cold running water and dry well with paper towels. Score the fish several times on each side, cutting down as far as the bone. This will ensure that the fish will cook evenly. Salt the fish inside and out, rubbing well into the skin. Place the fish on a plate and leave to stand for 40 minutes.

2 To make the soy-ginger dip, place the soy sauce, sugar, and ginger in a stainless steel saucepan. Simmer for 2–3 minutes, strain, and cool. To make the Japanese horseradish, measure the Wasabi powder into a small cup, add the water, and stir to make a stiff paste. Shape into a neat ball and place on a heap of shredded carrot.

3 Wash the fish in plenty of cold water to remove the salt. Secure each fish in a curved position before grilling. To do this, pass two bamboo skewers through the length of the fish, one above the eye and one below.

4 Preheat a broiler or barbecue to a moderate temperature and cook the fish for 10–12 minutes, turning once. It is customary to cook the fish plainly, but you may like to baste the skin with a little of the soy-ginger dip halfway through cooking.

EGGPLANT WITH SESAME CHICKEN

Nasu Hasami-age

Young vegetables are prized in Japan for their sweet, delicate flavor. Here, small eggplant are stuffed with seasoned chicken.

SERVES 4

Ingredients
6oz chicken, breast or thigh, skinned
1 scallion, green part only, finely chopped
1 tbsp dark soy sauce
1 tbsp Mirin, or sweet sherry
½ tsp sesame oil
¼ tsp salt
4 small eggplant, about 4in long

1 tbsp sesame seeds
all-purpose flour, for dusting

Dipping sauce
vegetable oil, for deep-frying
4 tbsp dark soy sauce
4 tbsp Dashi, or vegetable stock
3 tbsp Mirin, or sweet sherry

1 To make the stuffing, remove the chicken meat from the bone and grind it finely in a food processor, for about 1–2 minutes. Add the scallion, soy sauce, Mirin or sherry, sesame oil, and salt.

2 Make 4 slits in the eggplant so they remain joined at the stem. Spoon the ground chicken into the eggplant, opening them slightly to accommodate the mixture. Dip the fat end of the stuffed eggplant in the sesame seeds, then dust in flour. Set aside.

3 For the dipping sauce, combine the soy sauce, Dashi or stock, and Mirin or sherry. Pour into a shallow bowl and set aside.

4 Heat the vegetable oil in a deep-fryer to 385°F. Fry the eggplant, 2 at a time, for 3–4 minutes. Lift out with a slotted spoon onto paper towels.

JAPANESE RICE AND SUSHI RICE

Sushi-meshi

The Japanese prefer their rice slightly sticky so that it can be shaped and eaten with chopsticks. Authentic Japanese rice can be difficult to obtain in the West, but may be replaced by Thai or long-grain rice, washed only once to retain a degree of stickiness.

YIELDS 2LB COOKED RICE

Ingredients
12oz Japanese, Thai, or long-grain rice
5 cups boiling water
1 piece giant kelp, 2in square (optional)

Dressing
3 tbsp rice vinegar or distilled white vinegar
3 tbsp sugar
2 tsp sea salt

1 If using Japanese rice, wash several times until the water runs clear. Wash Thai or long-grain rice only once and drain well. Place the rice in a large heavy saucepan, cover with the measured amount of water and the kelp, if using. Stir once and simmer, uncovered, for 15 minutes. Turn off the heat, cover, and stand for 5 minutes more to allow the rice to finish cooking in its own steam. Before serving, the rice should be fluffed with a rice paddle or spoon. This rice is a Japanese staple.

2 To prepare sushi rice, make the dressing, by heating the vinegar in a small saucepan, with a lid to keep in the strong vapors. Add the sugar and salt and dissolve. Allow to cool. Spread the cooked rice onto a mat or tray and allow to cool.

3 Pour on the dressing and fluff with a rice paddle or spoon. Keep covered until ready to use.

BATTERED FISH, SHRIMP AND VEGETABLES

Tempura

Tempura is one of the few dishes brought to Japan from the West. The idea came via Spanish and Portuguese missionaries who settled in southern Japan in the late sixteenth century.

SERVES 4–6

Ingredients
1 sheet nori
8 large uncooked shrimp tails
6oz whiting or monkfish fillet, cut into fingers
1 small eggplant
4 scallions, trimmed
6 shiitake mushrooms, fresh or dried
all-purpose flour, for dusting
vegetable oil, for deep-frying
fine salt, to sprinkle
5 tbsp soy, or Tamari sauce, to serve

Batter
2 egg yolks
1¼ cups ice water
8oz all-purpose flour
½ tsp salt

Deveining shrimp

All raw shrimp have an intestinal tract that runs just beneath the outside curve of the tail. The tract is not poisonous but can taste unpleasant. It is therefore best to remove it.

1 Peel the shrimp tails leaving the tail part attached.

2 Score each shrimp lightly along its length, exposing the tract. Remove the tract with a small knife.

1 Cut the nori into ½in strips, 2in long. Moisten one end of the nori with water, and wrap around the tail end of each shrimp. Skewer the shrimp through their length to straighten them. Skewer the fillets of white fish and set aside.

2 Slice the eggplant into neat sections, sprinkle with salt, layer on a plate, and press lightly with your hand to expel the bitter juices. Leave for 20–30 minutes, then rinse under cold water. Dry well and place on bamboo skewers. Prepare the other vegetables on skewers and set aside.

3 The batter should be made just before it is used. Beat the egg yolks and half the ice water together in a bowl, sift in the flour and salt, and stir loosely with chopsticks without mixing into a dry paste. Add the remainder of the water and stir to make a smooth batter. Avoid overmixing.

4 Heat the vegetable oil in a deep-fryer or wok, fitted with a wire draining rack, to 350°F. Dust the fish and vegetables in flour, not more than 3 at a time. Dip into the batter, coating well, then fry in the hot oil until crisp and golden, for about 1–2 minutes. Drain well, sprinkle with fine salt, and drain on paper towels before serving with a soy or Tamari dipping sauce.

STRAW NOODLE SHRIMP IN A SWEET GINGER DIP

Age-mono

Shrimp are a popular feature in Japanese cooking. Rarely are they more delicious than when wrapped in crispy noodles and seaweed.

SERVES 4–6	2 sheets nori	**Dipping sauce**
Ingredients	12 large fresh shrimp tails, peeled and deveined	6 tbsp soy sauce
3oz Somen noodles, or vermicelli	vegetable oil, for deep-frying	2 tbsp sugar
		1 piece fresh ginger, ¾in long, grated

1 Cover the Somen noodles, if using, with boiling water and soak for 1–2 minutes. Drain and dry thoroughly with paper towels. Cut the noodles into 3in lengths. If using vermicelli, cover with boiling water for 1–2 minutes to soften. Cut the nori into ½in strips, 2in long, and set aside. To make the dipping sauce, bring the soy sauce to a boil with the sugar and ginger. Simmer for 2–3 minutes, strain, and cool.

2 Line up the noodles or vermicelli on a wooden board. Roll the shrimp in the noodles so that they adhere in neat strands. Moisten one end of the nori and secure the noodles at the fat end of the shrimp. Set aside.

3 Heat the vegetable oil in a deep-frying pan, or wok fitted with a wire draining rack, to 350°F. Fry the shrimp in the oil, 2 at a time, until the noodles or vermicelli are crisp and golden.

4 To finish, cut through the band of nori with a sharp knife exposing a clean section of shrimp. Drain on paper towels and serve with the dipping sauce in a small dish.

SWEET POTATO AND CHESTNUT CANDIES

Okashi

It is customary in Japan to offer special bean paste candies with tea. The candies tend to be very sweet by themselves, but contrast well with Japanese green teas; in particular, large-leaf Sencha and Banch.

MAKES 18

Ingredients
1lb sweet potato, peeled and roughly chopped
¼ tsp salt
2 egg yolks

7oz sugar
4 tbsp water
5 tbsp rice flour or all-purpose flour
1 tsp orange flower or rose water (optional)
7oz canned chestnuts in heavy syrup, drained
superfine sugar, for dusting

2 strips candied angelica
2 tsp plum or apricot preserves
3–4 drops red food coloring

---

3 To prepare the chestnuts, rinse away the thick syrup and dry well. Roll the chestnuts in superfine sugar and decorate with strips of angelica. To finish the sweet potato candies, color the plum or apricot preserves with red coloring and decorate each one with a spot of color. Serve in a Japanese lacquer box or on an open plate.

1 Place the sweet potatoes in a heavy saucepan, cover with cold water, and add the salt. Bring to a boil and simmer until the sweet potatoes are tender, for about 20–25 minutes. Drain well and return to the pan. Mash the sweet potatoes well, or force through a fine strainer. Place the egg yolks, sugar, and water in a small bowl, then combine the flour and orange flower or rose water if using. Add to the purée and stir over a gentle heat to thicken for about 3–4 minutes. Transfer the paste to a tray and cool.

2 To shape the sweet potato paste, place 2 tsp of the mixture into the center of a wet cotton napkin or handkerchief. Enclose the paste in the cotton and twist into a nut shape. If the mixture sticks, ensure the fabric is sufficiently wet.

Cook's tip

Sugar-coated chestnuts will keep for up to 5 days at room temperature, stored in a sealed box. Sweet potato candies will also keep, sealed and refrigerated.

INDEX

STOCKISTS AND SUPPLIERS

United States
Arizona
Kempo Oriental Market 5595 East 5th Street, Tuscon, Arizona, 85711, (602) 750-9009

Massachusetts
Yoshinoya 36 Prospect Street, Cambridge, Massachusetts, 02139, (617) 491-8221

Minnesota
M.F. Oriental Food 747 Franklin Avenue, Minneapolis, Minnesota, 55404, (612) 870-4002

New York
Katagiri Company 224 East 59th Street, New York, New York, 10022, (212) 755-3566

Siam Grocery 2745 Broadway, New York, New York, 10024, (212) 864-3690

Canada
Dahl's Oriental Food 822 Broadview, Toronto, Ontario, M4K 2P7, (416) 463-8109

Hong Kong Emporium 364 Young Street, Toronto, Ontario, M5B 1S5, (416) 977-3386

U-Can-Buy Oriental Food 5692 Victoria Avenue, Montreal, Quebec, H3W 2P8

ACKNOWLEDGEMENTS

The author and publishers would like to thank the following for generously supplying food products and equipment:

B E International Foods Limited
Grafton House
Stockingwater Lane
Enfield
Middlesex EN3

Thanks are also due to the following for their invaluable advice and assistance:

Mrs Duc Cung; Jane Wheeler; Yum Yum Restaurant, London N16